Working Class to College

The Promise and Peril Facing Blue-Collar America

Robert Owen Carr
with **Dirk Johnson**

This book is dedicated to

The Lockport Woman's Club

*...and to those who influenced me the most
in my Lockport days:*

Mrs. Murray
First and Second Grade, Reed School

Mrs. Robinson
Third Grade, Reed School

Robert Langlois
Social Science, Seventh and Eighth Grades, Ludwig School

Hugh Bitter
Superintendent of Schools, Ludwig School District

Margaret Taylor
English, Junior and Senior, Lockport Township High School

...and to Miss Enders, *the brand
new teacher who was forced to put up with this
problematic fourth-grade boy.*

TABLE OF CONTENTS

Bob Carr provides a clear picture of the college experience, good and bad, for children of working-class families, and in his philanthropic work he has found a way to make a real difference in these young people's lives. The University of Illinois is proud to claim Bob as our alumnus and pleased to be a partner in the Give Something Back Foundation program. ~Charles Tucker, Vice Provost, University of Illinois at Urbana-Champaign

Working Class to College *is compulsory reading for everyone concerned about the disparity of education in America, the high cost of college that leads to enormous student debt, and the need for clarity in career pathways for working-class students. Bob Carr lays out case studies and strategies that prove he understands these issues in a personal and insightful way. I highly recommend this book for college presidents, parents, policy makers, and anyone that is looking for reasons to be optimistic about the future of our next generation of students and wants to contribute to their success.* ~Michael J. Rounds, PE, President, Williamson College of the Trades

It's a rare man who acknowledges that his accomplishments are to be shared with others. Bob Carr is such a man. One person at one organization made a small gift towards Bob's education, but more importantly, Bob knew someone believed in him. Fast forward and thousands of kids are getting a college education, and more importantly they all know someone believes in them enough to invest in them. Bob is a special man, and this is a special story about appreciation, success and giving back. ~Peter Mallouk, JD, CFP, MBA – President and Chief Investment Officer, Creative Planning, Inc.

With a seamless mix of insightful advice, policy prescriptions, and touching real-world student stories, Bob Carr has provided a wonderful guide for both college-bound students and educational leaders. ~Dr. John Comerford, President, Blackburn College

There are few national priorities of greater significance for the individual and for the common good than the education of our young. Working Class to College *is a marvelous account of how Bob Carr gives back and invests in young persons who aspire to higher education opportunities.* ~Brother James Gaffney, FSC, President Emeritus, Lewis University

Robert Carr's personal experience is a truly inspirational tale of a working-class kid who beat the odds and succeeded in a remarkable way as a college graduate and entrepreneur with an unwavering dedication to pay it forward. Working Class to College *is a necessary piece that takes a hard-hitting look at a crisis currently facing our nation – the cost of higher education and student loan debt – while inspiring students and parents alike that the path to achieving a college degree can be possible even in the most seemingly impossible circumstances.* ~Eugene J. Cornacchia, PhD, President, Saint Peter's University

By exploring different paths to higher education and ways to minimize unnecessary student debt, this book delivers the important message of educational opportunity. Stories of hardworking students who overcame varied obstacles to achieve a college education with the help of GSBF powerfully illustrate this message while inspiring readers. ~Dr. Ali A. Houshmand, President, Rowan University

Robert Carr has experienced firsthand the power of higher education to transform lives. His personal story and this compelling book serve to inspire, challenge and uplift all who seek to have a positive impact on society and to create opportunity for individuals. ~Dr. Susan A. Cole, President, Montclair State University

As a first-generation college student myself, I found this narrative by Robert Carr truly inspiring and a must-read for parents, high school students, working adults, and yes, for college presidents and administrators. The real-life stories combined with facts to combat the myths surrounding the costs of a college degree are enlightening and the strategies to avoid the pitfalls a great resource for us all. Thank you, Mr. Carr, for this book and your life's work to provide opportunities for people to move from working class to college. ~Dr. Lynne Murray, President, Baker University

This is one of the best books that I have read which describes the problems facing students from working-class families who seek to go to college and what can be done to help them succeed. This is a well-written, interesting and inspiring book! ~Richard G. Clemens, Trustee, Williamson College of the Trades

ACKNOWLEDGMENTS

A book with this many case histories and this much research could only be accomplished with the support of many partners who were willing to offer their wisdom, experience, help and ideas.

We would like to thank our Give Back scholars for their contributions and for allowing us to use their personal stories in this book: Frances Brodeur (née Higgins), Shannon Keagle (née Stoffey), Noah Birch, Nicole Barker, Dominique Samuels, Dennis Cannon, Alejandra Arrué, Mark Washington, Fernando Erazo, Natalie Rigoni, Abby Turnbough, Taylore Gray, Michael Vitha-Nolan, Darnell Dail, Abbigail Suda, Emmanuel Mendez and Adrianna Martinez.

Other students and former students also shared their insights: Alex, Ally Gorecki, Jenni and Ken Bobicz, Michael Jordan, Emma Tragert, Lauren Silvers, Carly Ozarowski, Maddie Dwyer, Monika Dargis, Cole Byram, Stephanie FigPope, Lizette Delgadillo, Elizabeth Quick, Clark Johnson, Kassie Sturdyvin, Caitlyn Cordell, Leslie Juarez, Shaleeka Page and Johnny Page.

This book also drew on important insights of other books that highlight the unequal access to higher education: *Our Kids: The American Dream in Crisis*, by Robert Putnam; *College (Un)bound: The Future of Higher Education and What It Means for Students*, by Jeffrey Selingo; and *Where You Go Is Not Who You'll Be: An Antidote to the College Admissions Mania*, by Frank Bruni.

The tremendous staff of the Give Something Back Foundation made this book possible with their hard work and dedication to our students and their families and supporters: Steve Cardamone, Bob Tucker, Kevin O'Donnell, Kelly Dun, Rivka Tadjer, Kathleen O'Connor and Joshua Meekins (former Give Back scholar). The insights of Michael Parker, a member of our Board of Trustees, have been invaluable for the book and the scholarship program.

Our mentors are special people who volunteer their time to help coach and provide counsel and comfort to our rapidly growing population of scholarship recipients. We thank each and every one of these wonderful volunteers who are giving back themselves.

The high school principals, school counselors, and high school and college staff who help spread the word of our programs and who push their students to achieve high goals are where the rubber meets the road in recruiting our scholarship candidates. Without them, we could not do our job.

Without our college partners in Illinois, Delaware, New Jersey, Pennsylvania and New York, there would be no foundation. We thank these institutions, their leaders and their staffs for such incredible contributions to our work:

Lewis University, University of St. Francis, Blackburn College, Northern Illinois University, the University of Illinois, the University of Delaware, the College of New Jersey, Montclair State University, Rowan University, Saint Peter's University, William Paterson University, New Jersey Institute of Technology, Williamson College of the Trades and Mercy College.

A special thank you to Anne and Michael McMillan for making this book a reality, to Michael Roux at University of Illinois Press for his significant role in distribution and to Troy Johnson for his marketing support.

Dr. Rebecca Ginsburg assisted us in getting started with our initiatives to help children of incarcerated parents and Melissa Helmbrecht expanded our knowledge about these children and the significant needs of foster children. Warden Robert Balicki of Cumberland County Jail brought us into his facility so we could learn more from his staff and his inmates.

We also thank our past and future donors who provide a way for our successful programs to improve and to be sustained for many more years.

Finally, we would like to acknowledge the Lockport Woman's Club, the organization that inspired our work and gave us this opportunity to give back to so many others – who, in turn, will give back to thousands and thousands of others as the years go by.

PREFACE

My parents didn't want me to go to college. I grew up in a blue-collar family in a crowded little house in rural Illinois. I do not remember a book in the house. College, I was told, was for people who thought they were better than us.

Although they didn't use the word elitism, my father and mother saw higher education as a kind of snobby academic country club. In my dad's view, college was a place for soft, pampered kids and pointy-headed faculty intellectuals. It wasn't a place for the working class.

I am grateful that I didn't take the advice. More than fifty years have passed since I first stepped on campus at the University of Illinois, a bit anxious about competing with some very smart kids, but also exhilarated by the feeling of being freed from a trap. I was independent and now had the chance to chart my own path.

Going to college opened a new world for me. It broadened my perspective and changed the way I imagined the possibilities of life. I was in a big hurry. I earned an undergraduate degree in mathematics in three years. In my fourth year, I earned a master's in the new field of computer science. The college experience inspired a passion and sense of confidence that would ultimately lead to a career as the founder of a Fortune 1000 company that succeeded beyond my wildest dreams.

Looking back, I believe my parents were mostly just intimidated by the idea of college, a mysterious world where people spoke another language – indeed, dozens and dozens of other languages.

Unfortunately, many economically struggling families today still see college as beyond their reach – academically, culturally and financially.

It is my hope that this book nudges them to believe that they and their kids are truly college material.

Higher education can enrich lives and improve economic prospects like nothing else. Unfortunately, the college gap between affluent and financially strapped families is growing wider. In all kinds of ways, the playing field is unfairly tilted. Consider these disturbing truths from the US Department of Education:

Among kids with mid-level grades and test scores, those from the top income quartile are six times more likely to graduate from college than those with mid-level grades and scores from the bottom 25 percent. Some 80 percent of students from the upper quintile of income attend college, compared to 19 percent from the bottom quintile.

In what Harvard professor Robert Putnam has described as shocking, *High-scoring poor kids are now slightly less likely to get a college degree than low-scoring rich kids.*

That last fact, Putnam wrote in *Our Kids: The American Dream in Crisis, is particularly hard to square with the idea at the heart of the American Dream: equality of opportunity.*

Many start school and drop out, often because they and their families face financial adversity. There are now forty million Americans who started college, but did not finish. Personal accounts in this book reveal the quicksand that threatens those who took on loans and left campus without a degree. This is a phenomenon with frightening implications.

Media reports tend to focus on college graduates with huge debt, unable to buy homes and start families, or even live independently, putting a drag on the economy. But those with smaller debt – and no diploma – tend to fare even worse.

The trap of debt-and-no-degree – a problem that has largely been overlooked – is the reason so many former students default on comparatively small loans. Indeed, those with debt of $5,000 or less are six times more likely to default on loans than those who owe $40,000 or more. This seeming paradox is explained by the diminished career and income possibilities for those without a degree or vocational certificate. And for those who fail to pay the loan bills, the consequences can be disastrous and long-lasting. Defaulting on a student loan is tantamount to bankruptcy, whether it is less than $5,000 or over $50,000. It is worse, in fact, because student debt cannot be discharged in bankruptcy. Student loan debt can even mean the loss of Social Security payments.

As a senior in high school, I caught a break. I was awarded a $250 college scholarship from the Woman's Club in my hometown. The money helped toward college, and the boost in confidence was priceless.

Now it's my turn to lend a hand. I created the Give Something Back Foundation, which provides mentoring and scholarships to kids of modest means. These students are given the opportunity to graduate in four years without debt. Our foundation has paid for 850 scholarships and is on track to fund college for nearly 3,000 students who qualify for the Pell Grant, generally those who fall within the lower 40 percent of income. We are committed to changing lives – one working-class student at a time.

The students in our scholarship program have achieved a remarkable rate of success. More than 90 percent of our scholars have graduated from college in four years. We start early, selecting students in the ninth grade, and we set high expectations, both in terms of academics and character. The foundation of our program rests on these five requirements:

> *Enroll in the high school courses that will be adequate preparation for college, and remain in good academic standing. If a student is behind in reading or math, we help them with tutoring, and in some cases, summer programs that bolster academic skills.*

> *Take a full-time load every semester in college to remain on track to graduate in four years. Staying in college an extra year or two has worsened the debt crisis for millions of Americans. We recognize that students sometimes change majors, which requires taking extra courses. When necessary, we encourage students to take summer courses to stay on pace for graduation. We monitor the grade reports of our scholars after each semester or trimester to make sure they remain on track.*

› While in high school, take classes that qualify for college credit. This requires careful planning that starts in the ninth grade. It is not an option at all high schools and colleges. But for a very large number of cases, students are able to leave high school with a semester or full year or more of college credit. That makes it possible to graduate from college a semester or a full year early.

› Take as many classes as possible at a local community college, and select courses that will earn credit toward a four-year college degree. That way, students can get a head start on a bachelor's degree even as they work toward an associate's degree. We have seen students complete up to three years of university credit while still attending a community college. The Pell Grant, for students who qualify, will typically be enough to cover tuition at a community college, as well as books, lunches and transportation.

› Apply for as many scholarships as possible, paying special attention to those reserved for students who match certain backgrounds, needs and life experiences. Each of our students has an advisor assigned to help sort through the application process. Some parents of high-achieving students have been able to find schools that have provided scholarships that cover all tuition, fees and room and board. For more information, visit giveback.ngo

It is worth noting that the vast majority of economically struggling students come from families who work, often at jobs that are hard and dirty. For that reason, this book invokes the term *working class* – with its proud and noble tradition – in referring to students who come from families of modest or very scarce means.

I am now a wealthy man, but I remember what it was like to be short on money: the dread of unpaid bills, the threat of a car being repossessed, canceled credit cards, the notice of imminent home foreclosure.

For those fortunate and privileged enough to have escaped such experiences – for those who never had to worry about paying college costs for themselves or their children – the issue of educational opportunity affects them, too. It affects our society as a whole by stunting our workforce. People without education are more likely to go to jail or rely on government aid, programs paid from taxes. Wealthy kids, moreover, need to rub shoulders with more working-class students in colleges. They can learn plenty from each other.

Obstacles to going to college, as well as burdensome student debt, can create dissension and divisions in our society. It provokes a suspicion that the system works to benefit the comfortable and connected, and stokes notions among those who struggle financially that campus life is not designed for them. These are echoes from my working-class parents, bitter sentiments that have been growing unmistakably louder in America among those who feel left behind.

For the working class, it is a crisis that threatens to worsen as the economy continues to change in ways that reward education and punish those who lack schooling. Decent-paying jobs for those without a degree or a special skill, positions that were once widely available in the American economy, have all but vanished. Higher education, whether that means going to a university, a community college or a trade school, has become virtually imperative to earning a living wage.

For those who do not have a lot of money, this book explores the path to higher education and exposes some of the pitfalls along the way.

It is nothing short of shameful that so many smart, low-income high school students give up on the idea of going to college because they think they cannot afford it, or have not been shown the road map that can make it possible.

In planning for higher education, it is crucial for young people and their parents to remain open to many options, such as apprenticeships in high-skilled sectors. This path represents what Thomas Perez, as labor secretary, described as *the other college*. Some five million good jobs in the United States, from advanced manufacturing to information technology, go unfilled because employers cannot find people with the needed skills.

Hardworking students of modest means – including busy working adults who are trying to improve their career prospects by going back to the classroom – have too often been left in the dark about options and strategies, especially if they are the first generation to go beyond high school.

Students too often rely on advice that is inaccurate or based on old assumptions. It is not always smartest to go to Fancy U. Going to a more affordable school with a less glamorous name can lead to great careers, especially in the STEM fields – science, technology, engineering and math – with incomes as high as those who attended more expensive schools.

On the other hand, private schools should not automatically be ruled out as financially prohibitive. A top financial aid consultant, who assists students in the Give Something Back Foundation, notes that some private schools have big endowments and financial aid packages that can make college more affordable than going to a local public institution. Unless a student comes from a very affluent family, almost no one pays the sticker price.

This book charts ways students can reach higher education, whatever the obstacles. These pages reveal inspiring accounts of many students who grew up with little money or faced other obstacles – teenage pregnancy, the foster care system, citizenship status, the loss of a parent to death, abandonment or incarceration – but who heroically found a way to college and then the commencement stage, and ultimately, a great career.

It is possible to go to college without going broke. And for those who have been told that college isn't for them – whether they hear it from an authority figure, as I did, or from that inner voice of pessimism – they should ignore it.

Working-class kids need college. And colleges need them.

– roc

CHAPTER ONE

THE TRAP OF DEBT AND NO DIPLOMA

As Alex walked across the college commencement stage in Massachusetts, her mother and grandmother were perched proudly in the audience, beaming about her academic achievement.

Alex had seemingly beaten the odds. Her childhood, after all, had not been the easiest. She had been born to a young, unmarried mother, and she never knew her father. Raised by her grandparents, she grew up working-class in a little town in the rural Midwest. Most of the other families were nuclear and stable, or so it appeared. And she was a mixed-race girl in a predominantly white community. She sometimes had difficulty figuring out quite where she fit.

Nobody questioned her smarts. She excelled in the classroom and took home plenty of honors. With her academic talents, she gained admission to a highly respected private university on the East Coast.

From the start, Alex had worried about the big price of tuition and the hefty debt she would accrue. But her high school counselors told her not to worry about the money.

You're investing in yourself, she was told. *It's not like you're borrowing to buy an expensive new car or something.*

Going off to college in a diverse and cosmopolitan city would be a fresh start. She jumped at the chance. She majored in political science and international relations and earned high marks in the classroom. She studied abroad in Egypt and Syria. She dreamed of working in politics or government in Washington, perhaps on Capitol Hill, or maybe for an organization that focused on affairs in the Middle East.

For Alex's graduation, her mom and her grandmother had made the long trip from the cornfields to the big city near the Atlantic Ocean. They cheered and grew emotional when they heard Alex's name echo on the loudspeaker as a university graduate.

But Alex was keeping a painful secret.

She had not graduated. She had fallen short of credits for completion of a degree. The school had allowed Alex to participate in the commencement ceremony with the understanding that she would finish her degree requirements during the next semester.

But the next semester never came.

Years have passed since that commencement day when Alex, unable to tell the truth, had feigned a smile of academic triumph.

To this day, nobody in my family knows, she said in confidence, breaking into tears. *I didn't want to let my grandparents and my family down. They were really proud of me. I feel a lot of shame.*

In her senior year of college, she had become fixated about carrying debt of more than $80,000. The economy was still weak from the global economic crisis. How was she ever going to repay her loans?

And she had fallen behind in school. Working three jobs, she started to lose her way in the classroom, and she ultimately became overwhelmed. She was struggling mightily on the capstone project for her major. With everything weighing on her, Alex tanked. She bombed in two of her classes and ended up receiving Ds in both. Those poor marks brought a relatively lofty grade point down to a 3.0.

Completing the project and earning a degree would require staying in school for at least another semester. And it would come with a price tag of tens of thousands of dollars for tuition, books, room and board and living expenses. There was simply no money for that.

The pressures of life had begun to feel like a tightening noose. Some friends feared that she might take her life.

Alex didn't feel like she could talk about her plight with her family. They were so proud that she would be graduating. She couldn't bear to disappoint them.

She knew that her grandparents had dug into their retirement accounts to help with her school costs. They had co-signed on some of her loans. She couldn't think of asking them to give any more. And the truth was, they didn't have any more to give. Her grandparents were headed for bankruptcy.

After the charade of graduation, Alex moved home. Her grandparents would soon lose their home to foreclosure.

They had purchased a house in Florida, and were hit hard when the housing bubble popped. Alex knew that their economic downfall wasn't caused solely by helping with her college costs.

But it sure didn't help, she said. *And I feel so, so guilty.*

After her grandparents lost their home in Florida, they returned to the rural Midwest and rented an old farmhouse. Alex joined them and took a job at a nearby college, doing clerical work in an office that recruited law school students. She earned barely more than the minimum wage. With her monthly student loan payments of about $600, she could not afford to live on her own.

To this day, her grandparents, her mom and her two younger half-brothers all think she graduated from college.

As Alex saw it, there was no way to rectify the problem, since she could never afford to go back to school and complete the necessary work.

So why tell the truth? It would only cause more worry for the people she loved.

Alex was living a lie. And it was nearly swallowing her alive.

Some forty million Americans owe money for college loans–a sum now exceeding $1.3 trillion – more than automobile or credit card balances – according to a study by the Federal Reserve Bank of New York. The debt load has doubled in the last decade, as some 70 percent of graduates in the class of 2016 left the classroom with outstanding loans. According to an analysis by the *Wall Street Journal*, the average debt now tops $37,000, and weighs heavily on working-class students. Families with incomes of less than $40,000 are more than twice as likely to turn to college loans.

With so many new graduates leaving school with such big debt, some commencement speakers have been known to invoke a gallows humor in wishing them bon voyage – to their parents' basements.

A dramatic and deeper wrinkle in the crisis, and one that garners much less attention, is the huge number of students, like Alex, who borrow and later drop out of school. An Indiana University study found that thirty-one million Americans who started school in the past twenty years did not graduate. They have debt, but no diploma. It is a double whammy that reveals the dark side of the college dream.

A whopping 54 percent of students borrowing federal loans at public universities fail to graduate within six years. The ratio is only marginally better at private nonprofit colleges, where 45 percent of indebted students are unable to earn a degree within six years.

Those startling and dismal numbers were revealed in a 2016 study by the Washington-based think tank, Third Way. The numbers underscore how millions of young people are beginning their adult lives lacking a college degree and weighed down by a financial albatross.

The most common cause for students leaving school before they graduate: a lack of money.

That is the number one reason our students give when they drop out, Beatriz Gonzalez, vice provost for the University of La Verne in California, told the *New York Times*.

While the average college debtor in the US leaves campus owing about $37,000, some accrue debt of more than $100,000. The jaws of the debt trap slam hardest on those who leave campus without a diploma. As in Alex's case, they find themselves unable to qualify for the degree-required, higher-income jobs needed to cover monthly student loan payments and living expenses. The problem is especially acute for those from blue-collar backgrounds, who tend to lack financial help from parents or other relatives.

Going from the working class to college – and making it to commencement – is a steep hill to climb. According to the US Department of Education, the gap between rich kids and lower-income kids in completing college was thirty-nine percentage points a generation ago. Now it is a difference of fifty-one percentage points.

A 2014 White House report, *Increasing College Opportunity for Low-Income Students*, observed that half of all people from high-income families have a bachelor's degree by the age of twenty-five, compared to fewer than one in ten people from low-income families.

In *Our Kids*, Robert Putnam points to an especially unfair fact of life in economic class and higher education:

Lower-income students with top grades and test scores in high school are *less likely* to earn a college degree than are the relatively wealthy students with poor grades and test scores.

Many lower-income students, often the first-generation college-bound, give up even before they start. These are students who are accepted to college in the spring of senior year of high school and never make it to a single college class in the fall.

They're stymied by tuition sticker shock, Kafkaesque paperwork requirements and a quiet, corrosive feeling that they don't belong, according to a 2016 summary in the *Hechinger Report*, which analyzes education policy.

Their affluent peers are much more likely to have parents who attended college and can offer guidance. They can also supply them with a credit card for incidental expenses, like going out for a pizza with classmates, the kind of bonding rituals that can ward off homesickness and feelings of isolation.

Paradoxically, even college financial aid has been tilting in favor of the wealthier students. According to the New America Foundation, a nonpartisan think tank, the biggest shift in financial aid in the last twenty years has been from the disadvantaged to the affluent.

Colleges have been spending more money on merit aid, often doling out scholarships to students whose families do not need the help, and devoting less money to need-based grants, according to the New America report, *Undermining Pell: How Colleges Compete for Wealthy Students and Leave the Low-Income Behind*.

Stephen Burd, the author of the report, contends that colleges have turned to a *relentless pursuit of prestige and revenue*. Desperate to enhance the overall student profile that can help translate to a higher spot in the *US News and World Report* rankings, colleges are using endowment money to lure students with the highest grades and test scores. These prospects are most likely to be found in the affluent zip codes with schools oriented to college prep and families who have the money to hire tutors for help with the SAT and ACT college entrance exams.

Wealthier kids often get a boost in the application process just for being wealthier. Except for the relative handful of schools that are now need-blind, separating admission decisions from financial circumstances, colleges openly acknowledge that they consider a family's ability to pay in choosing among applicants.

For working-class kids, it can seem that the deck is stacked against them.

Starting in kindergarten, and even before, affluent kids typically go to highly regarded schools. Those raised in economic comfort have more opportunity to participate in the expensive extracurricular activities that enhance resumes. From grammar school onward, they are more likely to be afforded tutors when needed.

Even minor differences in scores on the SAT or ACT can help tip the scales with admissions offices, so affluent parents spend lavishly – sometimes thousands of dollars – for one-on-one tutoring to prepare their children for the college admission exams.

For those of modest means, the price of the test alone – the SAT costs more than $50 – can stress a tight budget. And they are hard put to pay the hundreds of dollars to take the test multiple times, as many wealthier students do, in hopes of bumping up their scores.

Students of modest backgrounds who are offered admission, meanwhile, often receive financial aid packages with an Expected Family Contribution that is far beyond their means. The packages often arrive just weeks before students and families must decide whether to enroll in a school. As a consequence, decisions are often made in a hurried, uninformed, and frequently, emotionally charged atmosphere.

Many of these students, the New America report concludes, *are left with little choice but to take on heavy debt loads, or engage in activities that lessen the likelihood of earning their degrees, such as working full-time, or dropping out until they can afford to return.*

Even before college costs, blue-collar family budgets are squeezed. According to a Federal Reserve Board survey, nearly one-third of adults, some seventy-six million people, reported they were either *struggling to get by* or *just getting by*.

Nearly half of all respondents in the study said they would not be able to pay for an unexpected expense of $400, or that they would need to borrow or sell something to cover the bill. Almost 40 percent of American children spend at least one year in poverty before they turn eighteen, according to the Pew Research Center. For black children, three-quarters are poor at some point during childhood.

The surest ticket to financial security is higher education. That might mean a bachelor's degree, a two-year associate's diploma earned at a community college, or certified training in a trade or skill. In today's advanced manufacturing – a sector that is far more sophisticated than the old assembly line – some 5.1 million jobs are currently going unfilled for lack of applicants with adequate technical education, according to the US Department of Labor. In the building trades, meanwhile, contractors complain about shortages of carpenters and other skilled craft workers.

There has been a lot of loose talk and errant assumptions in recent years about whether college is still worth it. A survey by Google asked whether the jobless rate among people aged twenty-five to thirty-four was higher among college graduates or non-graduates. A majority guessed that college graduates had the higher unemployment rate. They were wrong. The unemployment rate for those without a college degree was more than three times higher than the unemployment rate for those with a diploma.

The share of jobs requiring a college degree – now 65 percent of all positions in the workforce – grows larger each year.

We are far from reaching the place where a college degree is simply, as some cynics put it, *just what a high school diploma used to be.* Only one-third of young people will earn a college degree. And it pays off for them. A person with a bachelor's degree, according to the US Department of Education, earns an average of nearly $1 million more than a non-graduate over a working career.

On both the left and right ends of the political spectrum, the education class divide and the student loan burden, along with the disappearance of decent-paying jobs that once required no higher education – have contributed to a stirring of fear and frustration among working-class families.

It can seem to some that the implicit social contract of democracy – *my kids can do better than me* – has been broken.

The children of blue-collar America need a fairer shot at the promise of the enrichment of higher education and the path to greater economic stability. And the nation needs more college graduates – future civic and business leaders – who know what it's like to grow up in households that know struggle.

Efforts to help working-class kids find their way to college – and commencement – are often simplistically viewed, *New York Times* columnist Frank Bruni keenly observed, as *do-gooder favors* to lower-income students.

Hardly, Bruni scoffed. *It's a favor to us all. It's a plus to richer students who are exposed to a breadth of fresh perspectives that lies at the heart of the truest, best education. With the right coaxing, and a mixing on campus, they become more fluent in diversity, which has professional benefits as well as civil and moral ones. It's a win for America and its imperiled promise of social mobility.*

In a globalized and increasingly technological economy, America is hungry for talent from every region – urban, suburban and rural. We need the mettle, skill and creative gifts of every demographic group, whether a student traces the family lineage to arriving on the Mayflower or a slave ship, docking at Ellis Island or wading across the Rio Grande.

I am a product of the working class. I grew up in a home with more troubles than money. I am a wealthy man today, but I know vividly what it was like to be behind in my bills. I remember once begging the repo man with a tow truck to let me keep my car. I know what it's like to open a letter declaring that my home would be foreclosed and that my family's furniture would be put into the street 'next Tuesday morning' if my house payments were not brought up to date.

Back when I was twenty, I remembered asking myself: *If I am lucky enough to live to be sixty or seventy or ninety, will I be proud of the life I have led? Will I respect the values revealed by the priorities I have chosen?*

In my early fifties, my business venture finally did blossom in a big way. I had finally *made it* financially. I asked myself another question: *What do you do when you have more money than you really need?*

I didn't need a yacht or a string of sports cars or another vacation home or a private jet. Instead, I wanted to make a difference and repay a good turn that went back to my own high school days. I wanted to help more working-class kids be able to reach college and graduate without the burden of debt.

It is my goal to help finance at least 3,000 scholarships for kids from modest means, as well as provide mentoring and other support until they graduate. Thus far, nearly 1,000 scholarships have been funded. The scholarship and mentoring program has helped students in Illinois, New Jersey, Pennsylvania, Delaware and New York, with plans to expand rapidly throughout the country.

A majority of these scholarships go to kids who are first-generation college-bound. Some are first-generation American. More than a few have watched a mother or father die. Others have seen a parent go to prison. Some have never met their dads. These are students who have known hardship and adversity at an early age.

As a teenager, I caught a break. These kids deserve a break, too.

This is the story of the Give Something Back Foundation.

CHAPTER TWO

THE POWER OF GETTING A BREAK

More than fifty years ago, when I was a senior at Lockport Township High School, I was surprised to learn that I had been named a $250 college scholarship winner by the local woman's club.

I hadn't applied for the prize. I had never even heard of the Lockport Woman's Club. While I was a good student, I wasn't at the very top of my class. There were plenty of kids smarter than me.

I have a pretty good hunch that I was recommended for the award by a high school guidance counselor who was familiar with the circumstances in my home.

There were nine of us – six kids, my parents and grandma – living in a cramped, five-room house in a section of the countryside called Homer, seven miles outside of the Illinois town of Lockport in Will County.

Lack of money was only part of the problem. My father was often filled with booze and rage. My mother worked nights as a waitress to help support us. For many years, we had no television. For a long stretch, we were the only family I knew relying on coal for heat.

When I asked my mother once if we were poor, she paused for a long moment before answering.

Some people have more money than we do, and plenty of others have a lot less, she said. *We're about average.*

There was wisdom in her words. The difficulties I faced did not make me special. Everybody grows up with scars of some sort.

The Woman's Club award – both the money and the recognition – made me feel a bit differently about myself. It lifted my self-esteem. My work and abilities had been publicly recognized. In the eyes of someone, I had been judged as being worth an investment.

I remembered thinking:

If I ever have some extra money, I'm going to do something like this for someone else who could use a boost. I am going to give something back.

I enrolled in the University of Illinois in the fall of 1963, when John F. Kennedy was in the last months of his presidency and his life. It was an idealistic era, especially for the young. There was a sense that nothing was impossible.

I earned a bachelor's degree in mathematics in three years, and then a master's degree – in a new field called computer science – during my fourth year. And I did something that would be impossible for most kids today: I worked my way through college.

Tuition in those days was a flat $135 per semester. In today's dollars, that would be a bit over $1,000. In other words, the tuition was less than what some students now pay for books alone.

I washed dishes for the university's food service, at ninety cents an hour, and later managed an Arby's restaurant for two bucks an hour. At first, I worked twenty-five hours a week. It was enough to pay my room and board.

Between a grant for tuition, and a lot of hours spent working in kitchens, I was able to cover the cost of school. I was once even able to slip forty bucks to my father when he was desperate.

After graduation, I landed a job at the new Parkland College. I was quickly named head of the computer center and then I was elected faculty president. I was twenty-two. I also worked at the Bank of Illinois in Champaign. For someone not long out of college, I was making big money. When I turned twenty-three, my annual compensation was a whopping $30,000. In today's dollars, that would be a salary of more than $200,000.

I was determined to make a fortune. Barely twenty-six, I quit both jobs to strike out on my own as an entrepreneur. I was certain I would become a millionaire by age thirty.

Life, of course, can be humbling. There were times I thought about giving up on my dream of being an entrepreneur. But I never could figure out any other way to accomplish what was so important to me: to break the family cycle of financial hardship and bitterness about feeling shackled to jobs they hated. I didn't want my kids to grow up, as my siblings and I had, wearing nothing but hand-me-down clothes and brushing our teeth with salt because toothpaste was an extravagance.

I was determined to shape my own destiny and be my own boss. If I had been burdened with large student loans, it might have been impossible for me to strike out on my own. I simply might not have been as motivated to take a chance.

When my business did take off, after decades of struggle, and I was finally a man of means, I thought about the $250 scholarship award in high school – and what it meant.

I wrote a note of thanks to the club and enclosed a check for $5,000.

A gracious letter arrived from the club's president, thanking me and extending an invitation to attend the organization's annual banquet in 2002. So I flew back home to Illinois for the event.

As I sat in the audience, I thought more about the importance of the club's great mission and its modest resources. I also learned that it was, in fact, their 100th anniversary. When it was my turn to stand before the group, I surprised them by pledging a gift of $100,000 – a sum that I later learned amounted to three times their annual budget.

The money was to be used to fund college scholarships of $20,000 each for outstanding students in financial need at Lockport Township High School. It was the beginning of what would become the Give Something Back Foundation.

To qualify for a scholarship, the students were required to submit transcripts showing good grades. They supplied references from teachers vouching for good character. And they filled out forms, demonstrating that they were in financial need.

I sat in on the final round of interviews, along with my former wife, Jill, who played an important role in the program. We were joined by some school officials and representatives of the Woman's Club.

The kids were all dressed up. They knew there was a lot at stake. Many were scared to death.

One of the most nervous of the students was Frances Higgins. She looked like she might faint. At one point, a woman from the club encouraged her to relax.

It's okay, Frances, the woman reassured her. *Just breathe.*

In the interviews, we asked each student about their high school experiences, college plans and family circumstances.

Frances told us she had been accepted to Ohio State University. She had a real talent for numbers, and she had decided to major in actuarial science.

I asked Frances to tell me about her father.

I've never met him, she said simply. *He hasn't been part of my life.*

And your mother?

She worked three waitressing jobs, she explained, *and put herself through school to get a job as a med tech.*

When I shared with her that my own mom had been a night shift waitress, Frances seemed a bit more at ease. I think she realized that this business executive at the table, a man forty years her senior, was really just a working-class kid, too.

Frances had grown up in an apartment until high school, when her mom was finally able to afford to buy a modest home. It was a tiny place, an 800-square-foot house with two bedrooms and a single bathroom – not much bigger than a hotel suite. But her mom, Donna, was extremely proud to have become a homeowner. And she was right to be proud.

From the start, our scholarship panel had planned to select five students for scholarships. I was so impressed by these smart and honorable kids that I decided to pick six. Frances was one of them.

Another was Shannon Stoffey. As a little girl, she and her mom had been evicted from their home. They bounced around with relatives and friends. Her mom worked long hours as a cashier in a gas station.

I was surprised to learn that Shannon and her mom had ended up living in Lockport South Apartments. That was the same sad, dreary complex where I had lived so long ago, after a failed first marriage – a time when I was struggling to pay my bills.

When Shannon found out I had lived in the complex, she would later recall thinking, *He's one of us.*

I still am.

Not long afterwards, I was told about a young man named Noah Birch. Noah had already graduated from Lockport Township High School. He was attending the Illinois Institute of Technology on the South Side of Chicago, paying his school bills with loans.

Noah was six years old when his father died of cancer at age forty-five. As a little boy, he had stood at the hospital bedside and swabbed his dad's parched lips with moist sponges. Ever since then, he had dreamed of becoming a doctor and saving lives.

His widowed mom, Kathleen, was a social worker who earned a very modest salary. Noah and his older brother, Adam, grew up knowing they could not afford some things their friends took for granted. If the kids were going to make it to college, they would need to find ways to help themselves. That meant working, studying hard and applying for scholarships.

Noah did whatever he could to bring home a bit of money. He helped his brother with a paper route. He worked in a floral shop. He painted fire hydrants for the street department. And he was the valedictorian of his class of more than 700 graduates.

According to the rules of our foundation, the scholarships were earmarked only for current students at Lockport Township High School. Since Noah had graduated from the school the year before, he would not be eligible.

But when I heard Noah's story, I said, *To hell with the rules that I created!*

I phoned his mother to tell her that I was awarding a $20,000 scholarship for her son. It took me a while to convince her that it wasn't a prank call.

And then I called Noah and asked him a few questions about his life and school plans. He was willing to go into debt for his education. He would do whatever it took.

He told me about his dad. And he told me he wanted to become a doctor.

I told Noah I was going to invest in him. He would receive a scholarship from the Give Something Back Foundation.

Like a lot of the kids in the scholarship program, Noah has kept in touch. I will never forget the day that he called to tell me he had been accepted to the Stritch School of Medicine at Loyola University in Chicago.

Noah went on to earn his MD, as well as a PhD in molecular cellular biology. He chose the dual program so that he could conduct scientific research, as well as practice medicine. He wanted to study malignancies.

He is now a physician at Northwestern Memorial Hospital in Chicago. If anyone is going to find a cure for cancer, I think it will be Noah.

Frances, meanwhile, earned her degree in actuarial science at Ohio State. She and Noah were among the first group of scholarship winners in the Give Something Back Foundation. After the group graduated from college, I decided to take them on a trip to New York City.

These were young people, like me, who had been raised with the humble, working-class ethos of a small midwestern town. In down-to-earth places like Lockport, a common message is conveyed to kids: *Don't get too big for your britches.*

I wanted them to know that they could conquer the world.

I also understood the power of networking, which helps a person get a foot in the door, and maybe help seal a deal.

For the sons and daughters of waitresses, trades workers and office clerks – kids who did not attend a fancy prep school – navigating the world would have to mean finding their own way.

I wanted them to bond with one another and form their own sort of network. As I saw it, they could share contacts, trade tips, and build the kind of support structure that kids from wealthier backgrounds often use to establish careers.

The trip to New York was meant to open their eyes wide and consider the soaring possibilities. For most of them, it was the first time they had ever stepped aboard an airplane. Like me, they were products of a culture that generally cautioned against ever venturing to that scary Gotham City on the East Coast.

In Manhattan, we visited places the kids had seen on television or in the movies. We basked in the dazzling neon of Times Square. We strolled through Central Park. We watched the action in the New York Stock Exchange. We rode the boat to the Statue of Liberty. We ate hot dogs from a vendor on the sidewalk. And we sat in the Broadhurst Theatre on West Forty-Fourth Street and watched the Broadway hit play, *Mamma Mia*.

We became family. We grieved when Nicole Barker lost her dad, Dennis, to colon cancer, during her freshman year. Frances Higgins was a freshman when her mom was diagnosed with the cancer that would eventually take her life. Noah, of course, missed his father every single day.

Just starting out their adult lives, these were young people who could turn to one another for support. The foundation could also give them a hug when they needed one – and sometimes a nudge, if appropriate.

After Nicole's father died, her grades slipped at Eastern Illinois University. That's scarcely surprising. When you lose your hero of a dad, a rugged bricklayer who was not yet fifty, it can be difficult to concentrate in the classroom.

The college notified us about Nicole's plummeting grades. It was a condition of the scholarship to remain in good academic standing. My former wife, Jill, wrote a letter to Nicole that expressed deep sympathy. But Jill also reminded her that she would need to bring up her grades to keep the scholarship.

Nicole would later say that the letter was perhaps even more important than the scholarship money.

It was a pivotal point in my life, she later wrote. *I could choose to give up, lose the scholarship… or fight with everything I've got to get through it. Someone believes you're worth it. Prove it!*

Nicole would go on to become a successful chemist.

Shannon, who spent much of her childhood homeless, became an attorney.

For Frances, her dying mother struggled through chemotherapy, determined to live long enough to make the trip to Columbus, Ohio, for the commencement.

Frail, weak and suffering with pain, Frances's mom achieved her goal of watching her daughter become the first person in the family to graduate from a university. She died just six months later.

As Frances advanced in her career at a major insurance company in New York, she honored me by asking for guidance and advice.

She told me that she had found a company that, as she described it, *I loved and that loved me back.*

Not surprisingly, this talented young woman was soon being wooed by a competitor.

The interview turned into an offer that blew my mind, she told me. *It was three times what my mother made in the best year of her whole life!*

She explained how money could seem to trump everything else.

When you grow up having money challenges, she said, *the first question tends to be, 'How much?'*

In Frances's case, it meant a 40 percent raise that would catapult her to a six-figure salary.

But she had reservations. She had heard the owner of the company had a sleazy reputation. And she had serious doubts about whether the business would do the right thing by its customers.

I need an outside opinion, Frances wrote to me. *Not many people get to phone a Fortune 1000 CEO when they need advice. But the Give Something Back alumni do.*

An important reason she sought my advice, I was pleased to learn, went deeper than whatever success I've achieved in business. It was because I knew about coming from hardship.

I responded to Frances with a question:

Would you have the same passion in a sales role for this other company?

I was especially concerned with her misgivings about the ethics of the potential new employer.

No amount of money, I told her, *was worth working for a company that doesn't do the right thing.*

What's more, I was concerned that if she took the job, she ultimately wouldn't be as successful. If you don't believe in the product or company you're representing, it's going to be difficult to make a sale.

Frances passed on the offer. Some friends told her she was insane to be walking away from the big bucks.

I was convinced she was walking in the right direction.

Not long afterward, her company offered her a big promotion – and then yet another promotion. Frances would advance to a position that paid almost double the salary that had been offered by the competitor. Most important, she was still working for the company she respected.

It was always my hope that the scholarship winners would find ways to give back to others.

Not long ago, Frances and others came to me with the idea of pooling some of their money and contributing it to a scholarship for the Give Something Back program.

Their generosity was heartening. But I advised them to be patient: *All things in due time.*

I admire the philosophy of Carlos Castaneda. If you have just a bit of extra money, lend a helping hand to those close to you, and then expand your reach in concentric circles. A good place to start is the family.

In many ways, Frances gave back to her family by simply making it to the commencement stage. It brought immeasurable pride to her dying mother. And it served as inspiration to relatives that a college education was not beyond people of their economic station.

The message got through: *If Frances can do it, maybe I can, too.*

Her sister would go on to graduate with an associate's degree from Moraine Valley Community College in Illinois. Frances's brother-in-law earned a diploma at Moraine, too. Two of her cousins, meanwhile, would make it to Illinois State University.

The elder of the cousins, born to a teenage mom, had grown up largely taking care of her three younger siblings. She had so little contact with her father that she once bumped into a kid at a bus stop – unaware that he was her half-sibling. At home, there was no shortage of turbulence. Her mom experienced an ill-fated marriage, and then another.

Despite it all, the cousin made it to Illinois State, earned straight As in school and worked in a program that mentored kids. She also won admission to graduate school. Frances, who was over-the-moon proud, boasted that her cousin was on her way to earning the highest degree in the family.

The success of a scholarship is contagious. As Frances insisted, her own scholarship did not result in just one blue-collar kid going to college – *it should count for five.*

When I went to college, it was seen in my family as this really big deal, she said. *Now it's kind of expected that's what you're going to do – you go to college.*

Frances ultimately left her prestigious corporate job. She went to work full-time in the pursuit of giving back. In 2016, I hired her as director of philanthropy for the Give Something Back Foundation. The once frightened teenager who trembled in her scholarship interview had become a leader who could command a room with her poise and intellect.

In Frances's new professional role, she meets with generous businesses and individuals to explore the possibility of sponsoring scholarships for kids. When it comes to the soaring possibilities of smart and determined working-class kids, Frances is living proof.

At our annual Give Something Back Foundation dinner in 2016, Frances stood at the speaker's podium before a crowd of 899 people: friends of the program, donors, alums, administrators and board members.

But the focus was the large group of high school students who had earned a scholarship – bright kids who grew up with economic adversity, and sometimes domestic turbulence, and found a way to survive and thrive.

The young scholars were more than a decade younger than Frances, but she reminded them that they were kindred spirits:

I'm here to tell you that kids like you and me actually have a secret advantage. We have a grit and savviness that is natural when you have to figure things out on your own.

CHAPTER THREE

THE DANGER OF A DREAM SCHOOL

On a crisp morning during spring break, Allyson Gorecki,
a senior in high school, was visiting her grandparents down
the street when her cell phone began to ring.

It was her mother, Kathy, calling to tell her that some
important mail had arrived for her.

On the upper left-hand corner of the envelope, her mom
told her, the return address read: Marquette University.

Allyson clenched. Of all the colleges she had considered,
Marquette was her dream school.

Ally, as everyone knew her, had been a very good student
at Lockport Township High School, a middle-class town about
thirty-five miles southwest of Chicago. She had excelled in
Advanced Placement classes in English, chemistry and biology.
She participated in the French club and choir. She competed
in dance – her specialty was tap – and paid for team fees with
money from birthdays and Christmas gifts.

She went to mass every Sunday morning at St. Joseph
Catholic Church. She didn't use alcohol or drugs. She was a kid
with a purpose, driven to make a success in academics and a
career. Admission to a first-rate college would be a big step in

leaving behind her sleepy hometown and beginning to make her mark in the world.

Even though she had never visited Marquette, the school had sent her piles of brochures with statistics about the success of its students. Everything she had read and heard convinced her that it was the school for her.

Ally's family was Catholic, and it didn't hurt that Marquette was a school run by the Jesuits, an order of scholarly priests known for an independent streak and even a dash of charisma. The university's motto, 'Be The Difference,' seemed to capture the essence of a meaningful life.

Is it a big envelope, she asked her mom, *or a small one?*

As anyone knows who has ever trembled in anticipation of a college admission decision, a thin envelope usually means rejection or deferral. A big one signals triumph.

It's thick, her mom told her.

Open it! Ally shouted. *Open it right now!*

The envelope was ripped open and she could hear her mother's voice lift a decibel.

You're accepted! her mom declared triumphantly.

Ally soon visited Marquette and felt instantly at home. She loved the Gothic architecture, the historic statues and the urban bustle of Milwaukee. She met students who were smart and engaging, hip but not pretentious. She walked into the St. Joan of Arc Chapel, made the sign of the cross and gave thanks.

When she enrolled at Marquette, Ally studied hard to win good grades. She joined the college's varsity choir and was chosen to sing during a holiday celebration at the White House, where the Marquette kids performed *Lux Aurumque.* She made time to participate in Dance Inc. at Marquette.

A kid from a working-class family, Ally spent at least twenty-five hours earning money to help with expenses, holding down jobs as a nanny, a waitress and a clerk in the English department.

By the time graduation day arrived, Ally had been slapped with a bitter reality. Her student debt was overwhelming and her job options were scarce. In her field of speech pathology, she would need a master's degree, not just a bachelor's – and she and her parents were already swimming in debt.

She would need to move home. On the evening after the commencement ceremony, she rode through the darkness on Interstate 294 from Wisconsin back to Lockport, with her belongings packed in her dad's car. She felt as if she was headed in the wrong direction.

When Ally walked into the family's modest ranch house on West 146th Place, she retreated silently to her old bedroom. She looked at the wall to see a mural from *Beauty and the Beast*, a poster from childhood that now seemed almost mocking.

I was coming back to the same room I had when I was a seven-year-old girl, she said.

She was $125,000 in debt and she felt trapped.

The case of Ally Gorecki illustrates how the easy availability of big college loans can lead so many students into financial crisis. In many cases, students use the loan to pay to attend a Cadillac college, when a Ford would get them where they need to go.

As high school seniors, kids like Ally are suddenly empowered to make monumental financial decisions, taking on huge debt with an ease that makes the subprime mortgage heyday look like a model of restraint.

Like many students, Ally obsessed about a *dream school* – a place with a prestigious name that would wow peers and boasts plenty of alumni success stories – but also carries a breathtaking price tag.

Ally's mother and father, like many parents, were unable to foot the bills for college, but they were reluctant to stand in the way of a child's admission triumph. So both kids and parents end up taking out large loans for college.

As daunting as the loan repayment projections can be, the details in the financial aid package don't come close to telling the whole financial story. For starters, students are often unaware that an offer of financial aid for the freshman year might be significantly reduced in the following years, which can result in a student deciding to drop out or take on even bigger loans.

In the case of student debt, some of the usual remedies for financial liberation are nonexistent. Unlike other debt, student loans cannot typically be discharged in bankruptcy courts. That is why Suze Orman, the financial advisor, describes student loans as *the most dangerous kind of debt that is around today.*

Failure to pay college loans can lead to serious consequences. When college loans go unpaid for 270 days, borrowers go into default. A penalty of 25 percent can be added to the loan balance, even as interest continues to accrue. Being in default, or even delinquent, can be ruinous to a personal credit rating, and harm the chances of landing a job, as more employers today check credit history.

Unpaid debt can mean garnished wages. It can even lead to a loss of Social Security benefits. According to a 2015 study by the Federal Reserve Bank of New York, some 35 percent of people under age thirty with loans were in default.

Employers typically require college transcripts when making a hire, but many colleges will not release them for former students who are in default. Some schools refuse to admit any student already in default at another institution.

Being in default can also mean being ineligible for some government positions, and risking the loss of professional licenses, a punishment that befell forty-two nurses in Tennessee in 2011 whose loans were in default.

It comes as no surprise that freshmen in college report suffering high levels of anxiety, and even depression, because they worry about the big debts that are mounting.

College debt can even follow a person to the grave. Kevin DeOliveira was attending the University of Vermont when he was murdered in 2015. The student loan agency in his native New Jersey, soon afterward, demanded that his mother, Marcia, continue to make payments on his loan. By July of 2016, according to an investigation by ProPublica and the *New York Times*, the grieving mom had made eighteen monthly payments of $180. She had ninety-two payments to go.

Student debt is a drag on the nation's economy, even for those who don't owe a dime for a college education, by sapping the purchasing power of so many young people and their parents, too. Home ownership rate in the second quarter of 2016 slipped to its lowest point – 62.9 percent – since the US Census Bureau began tracking quarterly data in 1965. The drop is especially pronounced among younger adults.

How can college grads buy a car or make a down payment on a house – two of the biggest drivers of the economy – when they already owe what amounts to a mortgage payment to service their student debts?

The Pew Research Center has found that many people in their twenties and thirties are delaying marriage and putting off having children because they still face staggering college bills. Between 25 and 40 percent of borrowers in that age range point to student debt as the reason they have postponed the purchase of homes, vehicles and other big-ticket goods.

Janet Yellen, the chair of the Federal Reserve, has singled out the student debt crisis as an impediment to the housing market, especially among first-time buyers. The chief economist for General Motors, Dr. G. Mustafa Mohatarem, meanwhile, has cited student debt as one of the major reasons that millennials have not been buying more cars.

Other signs indicate that student debt is hamstringing the entrepreneurial spirit of young people. According to a *Wall Street Journal* analysis of Federal Reserve data, the percentage of younger people who reported owning part of a new business dropped to 3.6 percent from 6.1 percent between 2010 and 2013.

A lot of attention has been paid to young tech superstars in Silicon Valley who have grown fabulously rich by inventing a cool new app. But the real story is the crushing debt that is getting in the way of fledgling enterprises and potential start-ups for so many young people.

Mitch Daniels, the former Indiana governor who became the president of Purdue University, has warned about the consequences of these ominous trends:

The US, despite its proud protestations about how creative and risk-taking it is, has fallen in multiple worldwide measures of entrepreneurship, Daniels wrote in a 2015 essay in the *Wall Street Journal*.

Common sense says that the seven in ten graduates who enter the working world owing money may be part of this shift, Daniels noted.

The *Gallup-Purdue Index*, a large survey of college graduates, found that 26 percent of those who left school debt-free have started at least one business. Among those with debt of $40,000 or more, only 16 percent have done so.

Time is money, of course, and delaying graduation means both extra tuition and room and board expenses, as well as opportunity costs from the loss of wages that would be earned in the workforce.

Universities now typically measure graduation rates in terms of the percentage of students earning a degree within six years, not four. And researchers at Temple University and the University of Texas have found that two extra years on a university campus increase debt by nearly 70 percent.

Navigating the requirements for graduation in a particular major can be very confusing for a student, especially so for a first-generation student from the working class. The surest way to keep a student on track is face-to-face advising. But such advising is becoming harder for students to find. On average, there was one advisor for every 367 college students in the US, down from one for every 282 students in 2003, according to a survey by ACT and the National Academic Advising Association. The survey found that advisors were typically unavailable on evenings and weekends, and that waits for an appointment during business hours often stretched for weeks, according to findings published by the *Hechinger Report*, based at Columbia University's Teachers College.

We have a situation of almost completion by accident rather than completion by design, according to Davis Jenkins, a researcher at Columbia.

Some schools, including the University of Florida and Arizona State University, have implemented an online tool with color-coded maps that help keep a student on path and on time. When a student veers off course, a warning is sent in flashing red lights and a meeting is arranged with an advisor.

It is one smart way to cope to make the college experience more efficient and less expensive. Such assistance is keenly needed. Too many students now simply wander about, changing majors and taking more credits – and paying for them – than are necessary.

A bachelor's degree typically requires 120 credits. But graduates are racking up an average of 136.5 credits, according to the group, Complete College America.

Ally was one of those students who drifted off course. It took her five years to graduate. She had started school with an emphasis on pharmacy studies, but found – as plenty of students do – that she had chosen a field that simply wasn't in her wheelhouse. One of three college students changes majors, according to research at the University of California, Los Angeles.

She switched her career aspirations to speech pathology. It was a move inspired partly by the experience of family members who had overcome speaking impediments.

For Ally, gaining the proper credentials for a career in speech pathology, however, would require going to graduate school, a reality she said she came to realize late in the game.

Rather than seeing her go straight to graduate school – and racking up still more debt – her strapped and anxious parents urged her to *just get a degree in something.*

She graduated with degrees in English and psychology, with more credits than she needed. As Ally knew, neither of these were majors that typically had employers banging down the door.

And none did.

Monthly student loan payments, on the other hand, kicked in soon.

Ally would have preferred to stay in Milwaukee and work doing just about anything. But she didn't see that as a viable option. She could scarcely afford her monthly loan bill of $950 and pay rent, too.

So she went home. Despite being a Marquette graduate – a widely respected school with a strong national brand – Ally found herself working three minimum wage jobs. She took a position on the janitorial staff at her old school district in Will County. She signed up to wait tables at Chesdan's Pizzeria on South Bell Road in Lockport. And she found an opening for a dance teacher for children in the nearby Oswego Park District.

Her circumstances have become familiar to her generation.

More than half of 2014 college graduates under age twenty-five were either unemployed or working at jobs that did not require a college degree, and about one-third of adults under age thirty-one were living with parents. For the first time on record, more Americans aged eighteen to thirty-four were living at home than were living independently, according to a Pew Research Center study released in 2016.

Ally's parents did not charge her rent. And she was grateful. Living at home as a grown child, however, came with challenges.

If she visited a friend in the evening, a rare occasion, it could cause tension when she came home late. It was a difficult transition for a young woman who had grown accustomed to living on her own. It was an adjustment for her parents, too.

I'm not a bad kid, she said. *I'm not a 'let's go to the bars' kind of person. I'd rather get together and have a cup of tea or a bottle of water and watch a movie with friends. But my parents are very strict. You just feel like you're fifteen again.*

Ally planned to live at home for a year or two, send almost every penny she earned to the student loan collectors, and then go to graduate school. If everything worked out, she would have a master's degree – and college debt somewhere in the vicinity of $200,000.

For mothers and fathers who are sensibly rattled by the prospect of staggering college debt, it can be very difficult to tell a daughter or son to ratchet down their dreams – especially for a kid who has studied hard, worked hard, played by the rules.

When Ally Gorecki gained acceptance to Marquette, her parents were understandably proud of their daughter's achievement. They were also concerned about the cost.

With a household income in the $60,000 range, their means were limited. And they had two younger daughters who would soon be going to college.

Jim Gorecki remembers the discussion:

Her mother and I sat down with Ally at the kitchen table and said, 'You know this is very expensive. Is there some place closer? How about community college for a couple of years?'

He said Ally was 100 percent-focused on Marquette.

If I do everything right, she told them, *I should graduate with a job – and a good job at that.*

Okay, her father told her, *we'll back you all the way.*

Jim co-signed for many of her loans. He went on the hook for some $82,000.

Students and parents have very little time to make major financial decisions about taking out loans. At many schools, students have only about a month from the time they receive a financial aid offer to decide whether to enroll. That doesn't leave much time for emotions to cool or for families to do research.

The structure and terms of loans and repayment can be extremely complicated. For first-generation college students, navigating the financial aid process can be especially overwhelming. And when the bills come due, it can be even more confusing.

Jim Gorecki acknowledged being befuddled at times.

I don't have the money to hire a lawyer to put eighteen pages of terms and conditions into something a layperson can understand, he said. *I've spent days calling the bank and trying to work out a deal. But I know I'm only talking to one of 100 employees in a call center. And they're only able to tell you what the computer screen tells them to say. It always ends with, 'When can we expect your payment?'*

The circumstances caused Jim and Kathy to lose plenty of sleep. Ally had five loans. Consolidating could mean interest rates that would reach beyond 12 percent, a higher cost than a lot of credit cards. They considered mortgaging their house for money to put toward the college loans.

The student loan troubles have snared parents who have co-signed for children or taken on big debts through the Parent PLUS borrowing program. Many of these parents are consequently sinking deeper into debt at a time in their lives that they need to be saving for retirement.

For Ally, brown-eyed and slender, it often felt as if she was carrying a heavy load, along with a sense of embarrassment.

I sometimes feel like the cliché of the girl who couldn't make it, she said, *back in her hometown and working at the pub.*

When friends of her parents see her, she would gulp. *They approach with big smiles and ask, 'So, what are you up to?'*

She did not relish explaining her predicament, and she sometimes detected a hint of judgment.

Among those her age, she said, peers tended to be much more sensitive about asking probing questions. With so many young people underemployed, searching for jobs or struggling with debt, it is considered impolite to put someone on the spot.

There's sort of a pact, said Ally. *You just don't ask.*

As an emotional outlet, she wrote poetry and logged entries into a diary. She sometimes felt like giving up. On one particularly difficult day, she wrote simply: *I can't do this!*

But she pushed ahead.

If I don't keep moving, she said, *I'll fall apart.*

For transportation to get to work, she bought an old white Pontiac Bonneville, cashing in bonds that had been given to her as gifts when she was a child.

Despite her grueling work schedule, she spent almost every spare moment at a coffee shop studying for the Graduate Record Examination, the test needed to qualify for a master's program. With so much work and study, she would often rise at 5 a.m. and go full speed until 1 a.m.

When she took the GRE test, she scored well enough to be a competitive candidate for graduate school admissions – and a candidate for more student debt.

In too many cases, big student debt has derailed dreams, evoked a sense of betrayal and led to devastating consequences.

Jenni and Ken Bobicz, social workers with student debt in six figures, stayed current with their loans, but were left without money to pay other bills. They fell behind in their house payments, and eventually lost their home to foreclosure.

The burdens of college debt often go beyond imperiling a student. It can exact a painful toll on relationships within families.

For a thirty-year-old Ohio University graduate named Michael Jordan, it meant relying on his mother so often he felt humiliated and worried that she saw him as a burden. He acknowledged that he wouldn't blame her if she ran out of patience.

Michael was paying $850 a month for student loans that financed his bachelor's degree in English and German. After making his loan payment, he was barely able to support himself by waiting tables in restaurants.

He would even take a calculator to the grocery store, counting every cent to keep within his budget, and sometimes taking items back from the checkout line.

Even getting a flat tire – an inconvenience, to be sure, but not ordinarily a crisis – left him stranded, physically and financially.

I'm at a tire store and I'm calling my mom, he said, clearly embarrassed about imposing on his mother, yet once again. *But I literally didn't have enough money to pay the bill so I could move my car.*

It's not as though his mother, an elementary school teacher, had a lot to spare.

I know there are times when I call my mother, he said, *and she sees my name on Caller ID and just shakes her head and thinks: 'Oh, what now!'*

In many families, parents help a grown child who is deep in student debt, only to hear complaints from siblings. One man, unhappy about the family nest egg being used to pay his sister's loans, acknowledged telling his parents that he expected the score to be settled *on the other side.* In other words, he expected a bigger share of the inheritance.

Student debt can even ruin romances. It is common for parents to warn their adult children against getting hitched to someone with a lot of debt – whether it's credit card or student loans. And when people do get married, a load of student debt has the potential to cause bitterness.

Jana Lynch, writing in a blog post for *Student Debt Survivor*, explained that she knew that her boyfriend had borrowed to pay tuition for his master's education. She didn't ask questions about it at the time, she said, because she didn't think it was any of her business.

But then we got married, she wrote. *And our finances were combined. And his debt became my debt. And then I found out the number. And maybe I freaked out a little bit.*

She added, *I don't resent my husband's debt. I really don't. He did what he had to do in order to fund his education and I am proud of him for that.*

Unfortunately, plenty of people *do* resent the student debt that a partner brings into a marriage.

CHAPTER FOUR

THE CONFLICT BETWEEN STATUS AND COMMON SENSE

In the guidance office at Emma Tragert's high school, banners were posted in the spring for each college that one of the graduating seniors would be attending.

It is a common practice, meant to celebrate the accomplishments of students. Many other schools, after college acceptance letters (and rejection letters) have been mailed, earmark a day for students to wear the shirt of the school they have chosen to attend – or more to the point, the school that has chosen them.

However innocent or well-meaning, it is a not very subtle way of celebrating the students that have been accepted by the big name schools, and rubbing it in the noses of those who have chosen more modest routes. Imagine walking to class wearing the shirt of a humble community college, as many have done, and hearing the cascades of *Wow!* and *Awesome!* directed toward the students waltzing down the corridors in shirts from the nation's celebrity schools.

The message is pretty clear that going to the most prestigious college is what we're all about honoring, said Emma, *instead of honoring each student for making the choice that is smartest for that individual student.*

Emma's wisdom came the hard way. And she feared that her choice would keep her shackled for the rest of her life.

Planning to make a career as a book illustrator, she took a cue from the social pecking order and decided to aim for the most prestigious school that would accept her.

As she put it, *I wanted to go to the Harvard of the art schools.*

Emma was aware that the cost would be steep, but her parents assured her that she need not worry. Education debt was *good debt,* and in any case, they would be there to help.

And then the loans began to mount.

But the school wasn't the right fit for her. As someone who wanted to be an illustrator for children's books, Emma was looking for an art school with a practical and disciplined ethos. She wanted to learn a skill. Instead, the school took a more ethereal approach.

Rather than focusing on the craft of making art, Emma said students and teachers would spend a lot of time engaging in airy discussions about notions like, 'What is art, anyway?'

Taking a job to help pay the way through school, Emma worked in a coffee shop at the local bookstore. While serving a customer one morning, she suffered a burn from some very hot coffee that had spilled. She could probably have found a lawyer eager to file a suit. But she never gave that a thought.

It was my fault, said Emma. *I was tired and I just dropped the pot of coffee in my lap.*

She was hospitalized, and needed time to recuperate. She took some time off and moved home. As she recovered, she took a job in another coffee shop.

When it was time to go back to school, Emma decided to enroll instead at another school for the visual arts. It seemed like a school better suited to her career plans.

Emma worked hard and did well. She earned a place on the Dean's List.

There was a problem, however, with money owed to the first school. The portion her parents had promised to pay, it turns out, was never paid. The college refused to release her transcripts until it was paid a sum that exceeded $30,000.

For a while, Emma was upset with her parents for being irresponsible with the money and breaking a promise. But she worked through it.

They're the only parents I have, she said, *and I know they didn't want this to happen.*

As Emma saw it, she had two choices. She could borrow an additional thirty grand, and then some, to pay what she owed the college – or she could go back and start at zero, which would mean enrolling at a community college.

She supported herself as a babysitter and as a barista in a Swedish coffee shop in Brooklyn. She tried to do some illustration work – portraits of families, for example – and break into the art world without going the college route. But she knew that lacking a degree, as she put it, *could very likely mean I'll be a barista forever.*

Emma wished she could turn back the clock. She would have listened to her grandparents. While everyone else was waving away concerns about taking out big loans, her grandpa, a retired General Electric worker, cautioned her about getting too deep into loans. And her grandma was worried, too. Their warnings, unfortunately, were shrugged off.

I just thought, 'Oh, they're my grandparents,' said Emma. *They just don't know what it's like to be an artist.*

Her parents, meanwhile, carried a terrible sense of guilt about leading their daughter in the wrong direction, encouraging her to take out loans, promising they would pay a big chunk, and then letting her down.

They feel so bad, said Emma, *that they've been in therapy to try to deal with it.*

Lauren Silvers, an assistant professor at the esteemed University of Chicago with a PhD in literature, sadly resigned the academic world – doing what she loved the most – because a teacher's salary could not pay her huge loans.

The scholarly world had given her every reason to believe she should stick with her dreams of a career in academia. She was a top student at the University of California, Santa Cruz, where she majored in modern literary studies. She garnered still more accolades while earning her doctorate in comparative literature at the University of Chicago.

She scored triumphs in the rarefied world of academic publishing. Among other works, she authored, "Beyond the Senses: The Cenesthetic Poetics of French Symbolism" for the journal *Modern Philology*.

A native of the San Fernando Valley, she was a first-generation college student, one of the pioneers who navigated unfamiliar academic terrain without savvy advice from parents who have been through the process.

Her father and mother were in no position to offer any help in financial matters, either. Years earlier, they had lost everything.

For Lauren, staying in school meant working, scrimping and borrowing. As a student, she held several jobs, including full-time work through undergraduate school. But she still racked up student loans of more than $100,000.

While she grew anxious about her college debt, she said advisors would wave off her concerns:

'Don't worry! You'll have the rest of your life to pay it off.'

Lauren secured a postdoctoral position as an assistant professor at the University of Chicago. As her contract neared an end, she looked for a tenure-track position at a university, but such slots, especially in the literature field, are as scarce as hen's teeth.

She could have settled for a position as an instructor or an adjunct professor, a part-time teacher who earns perhaps $4,000 per class, joining the ranks of the low-paid workers who do a majority of the teaching on college campuses. Some 70 percent of the classroom instruction in American colleges is being done by this *contingent faculty*, according to the Association of Governing Boards of Universities and Colleges. A big share of these adjuncts makes less than some of the baristas in cafes that cater to the campus crowd.

With Lauren's student debt, earning such low wages would not be tenable. She wondered how others could do it. As she looked around at the nontenured teachers who were able to *hang on*, as she put it, she observed a vivid class divide.

What you'll find are people who are able to draw on other resources, she said, *whether it's their family, a spouse, a partner.*

For those without financial backing, it often means giving up on the academic world.

After spending many years in school and accruing a mountain of debt, Lauren abandoned her quest to become a professor, and took a job that brought her much less fulfillment, but a livable paycheck.

I beat myself up for thinking I could reach for the stars and follow my dreams, she said. *At least I've got my PhD. They'll never be able to take that away from me.*

Deep in debt in her late thirties, she gave up on more than a career in teaching. She was consumed by worries about her loans. She even ended a serious romance because she did not want to saddle a man she loved with her debt.

Debt was the first thing I thought about in the morning, she said. *And it was the last thing I thought about at night. It kept me from sleeping.*

Lauren left the academic world with a deep measure of bitterness. She no longer sees higher education as bastions of idealism.

Colleges, she said, *are really run very much like corporations.*

It is a fact of university life that is acknowledged by some academic insiders, even among those at nonprofit institutions.

There is an inherent conflict of interest at the heart of for-profit educational institutions, where the profit motive eclipses everything else, Carl Selkin, a former dean at California State University, Los Angeles, wrote to the *New York Times*. *Public and nonprofit colleges are increasingly falling into the trap of this spreadsheet mentality as well – depending more and more on part-time faculty members who may be well prepared and dedicated, but who must take on excessive workloads to survive.*

On the walls and gates of America's institutions of higher learning, there are plenty of phrases engraved in Latin. As Lauren Silvers could attest, perhaps another Latin phrase should be posted for incoming students: *Caveat emptor – Buyer beware!*

CHAPTER FIVE

WHEN THE MAJOR DOESN'T FIT THE BILL

College classrooms buzz with talk of arcane theories and intellectual abstractions. But it is the rare professor who spends much time discussing the likelihood of whether a particular major will lead to a job that can pay the bills.

Students deserve to be told more about realistic employment prospects and expected wages. How many jobs are available in particular fields and majors? What is the beginning pay?

If students choose to incur mountains of debt for expertise in fields that are esoteric or highly theoretical, as they have the right to do, they should be made aware of the market realities.

They should also be fully informed about the terms of the loans. Many students and parents are unaware that some loans start rolling up interest charges at the beginning of school, not the end. That means the loan balance will be even larger after graduation (or when a student drops out) than the sum borrowed to go to school.

Parents can help their kids avoid financial calamity by helping them understand the consequences of large, long-term debt and by encouraging them to consider reasonable options.

Parents, too, need to be wary of being swept away by notions of the prestige of fancy colleges and fashionable campuses.

In many social circles, unfortunately, it has become a version of keeping up with the Joneses. Sending a child to a pricey name college is a status symbol. But it's the kids who often get thrown under the school bus.

Students and parents alike need to be smart shoppers about the college choices, and plot strategies that realistically fit their financial circumstances. That can mean opting for a nearby, lower-cost school, or searching for those schools with large endowments and fat financial aid packages.

Pat assumptions can be dead wrong. Public schools are not always the cheapest route to higher education, especially as state aid has declined. Private institutions, in many cases, are in a position to offer very generous financial aid packages – often charging only a fraction of the rack rate.

And while most families are unaware of it, many colleges will consider negotiating costs, especially in cases where a student has an attractive offer from another school, or has exam scores that can help boost the admissions profile of an institution.

Anthony P. Carnevale, the director of the Center on Education and the Workforce at Georgetown University, makes it his mission to connect the dots between the ethereal academic experience and the concrete demands of the workplace.

Colleges are terrible at career guidance, said Carnevale, with a wince, speaking from his office on the idyllic campus in Washington, DC. *The typical message to students is, 'Explore! Find out who you are!' It's a wonderful experience. But it presumes that everybody is upper-middle class.*

Students from affluent backgrounds are far less likely to feel the burden and worry that comes with long-term debt. They also have the luxury of knowing they can make a mistake and survive, even take the time to switch career and academic directions.

Those from modest economic backgrounds have fewer resources, more debt and less time to devote to an expensive education. Compared to their prosperous peers, they are more likely to be fending for themselves. The margin for error is razor-thin.

One academic failure, one arrest, one grave illness in the family – any such setback can halt a college career, perhaps for good. As Carnevale put it, they are *one-and-done*.

With little or no financial cushion, working-class students need to be keenly aware of career financial realities when choosing a field of study, especially if they will need to repay heavy college loans.

Studying the Greek classics is enriching, but employers typically pay for specific skills that can be applied to a job.

Carnevale noted that while income inequality has stirred passionate debate, much less focus is paid to the *education inequality* that has driven and deepened the financial disparities.

In the smokestack economy of 1970, some 70 percent of American workers had a high school diploma or less, and most were doing fine. In today's economy, the *education have-nots*, as Carnevale has dubbed them, typically have much slimmer hopes of reaching the middle-class station that was once accessible to workers on the assembly line who did not have special skills.

Between 2010 and 2015, the nation produced 6.6 million jobs. The so-called good jobs – those paying the top 33 percent of wages – numbered 2.9 million. *Almost all of them,* 2.8 million, went to college graduates.

A person with a college diploma is on pace to earn an average of 84 percent more over the course of a lifetime, roughly $1 million, than a person with a high school education or less.

Nearly as important, the type of major explains wide disparities in income among the college educated. The Center on Education and the Workforce examined median salaries of 137 fields of study, and found that top-paying majors earn $3.4 million more in a lifetime than the lowest-paying majors (individuals with low-paying majors, on average, still outearn those without a college degree).

STEM fields were at the top in earnings. Majoring in petroleum engineering, for example, led to jobs with a median income of $120,000.

That could be expected. In an age of rapid technological advances, the demand for workers with STEM skills has outpaced the supply. That translates to plentiful job opportunities and higher salaries.

What was more surprising, however, was a 2016 report that found only narrow differences in the earnings of STEM graduates from the prestigious colleges and those who attended the more humble schools.

What we found startled us, according to the authors of the study by the *Wall Street Journal. For STEM-related majors, average earnings don't vary much among the college categories.*

For science majors, the analysis found *no statistical differences* in earnings between graduates from so-called elite colleges and those who attended middle-tier or less-selective schools. For engineering majors, the researchers found *only a marginally significant difference between* the top-tier schools and those considered much less prestigious.

What's going on? the researchers wondered.

For potential employers, the value of these skills trumped the importance of the name of the school. That's likely because curricula are fairly standardized. In other words, students are learning much the same concepts, regardless of the school.

Our findings are crucial for families to understand, the report added, *because chasing a prestigious STEM degree can leave students burdened with huge amounts of unnecessary debt.*

As an example, if a student chose to attend the University of Pennsylvania in the Ivy League, the average starting salary would differ by less than $1,000, *but the tuition difference would be over $167,000.*

For other majors, the prestige of the school did correlate to higher salaries. But those differences were not as stark as one might imagine. The biggest earnings difference was found among business majors. Graduates from the more prestigious schools earned 12 percent more than mid-tier graduates and 18 percent more than those from less-selective colleges.

For social science majors, graduates from more highly selective schools earned 11 percent more than their mid-tier counterparts and 14 percent more than those from less-selective schools. For education majors, the report found, the differences were 6 percent and 9 percent, respectively. In the humanities, graduates from more selective schools earned 11 percent more than those from less selective schools, but did not earn more than those from mid-tier schools.

As the study noted, the obvious and practical takeaway is that parents and students should really dig into the numbers. Sites like Payscale.com and CollegeScorecard.ed.gov provide statistics about earnings by college and by major.

Many families count on high school counselors and college professors to parse these numbers and wave caution flags when students pursue fields of study likely to land them in low-paying fields. Unfortunately, it often does not work that way.

Some for-profit schools have been rightly denounced as scams for pushing slick promotions that lure students with promises of prosperous careers that never materialize. Students at such schools default on loans at more than twice the national average.

But far too many of the 'respectable' nonprofit colleges have been culpable, too, in failing to communicate with students about the relationship between a field of study and career possibilities.

At one large midwestern university, a teacher of journalism— a field that has been shedding jobs for many years – confided that most of her peers are either clueless about the job market or are purists who see no place for mercantilist concerns in the noble work of education.

They've got their heads in the clouds, she said. *A lot of them don't get it. And they don't think they need to get it.*

For most people who are planning a career, money is scarcely the only thing that matters. Society would be much poorer without those who pursue good works for low pay. Social workers can help heal families in need of mending. The passion to work for an important cause, despite modest compensation, can be a gratifying way to change a bit of the world for the better.

But more than their wealthy classmates, students of humble roots might be advised to seriously ponder the severe limits and sacrifices such choices will mean. That's the view of Carnevale, the Georgetown economist who is himself a product of the working class in rural Maine. The virtuous *save-the-world* jobs, he said, are typically better suited for wealthier young idealists, those who can more easily afford the skinnier paychecks. In a financial crisis, the affluent can call home for help.

As a young man, Carnevale said he asked his mother, Frances, who knew plenty about economic struggle, for advice about his career direction.

Do what you want, she told him. *Just don't be old and poor.*

CHAPTER SIX

HASTY DECISIONS AT THE BUZZER

Students and families often wait until the senior year of high school before making a strategic plan for college – and that can lead to emotionally blurred choices that are unwise or unrealistic.

In the Give Something Back Foundation program, we sponsor a seminar open to all high school freshmen and their parents – whether they are selected for a scholarship or not – that gives them a pretty good idea about the costs at the colleges they are considering, and how much they can expect to receive in financial aid.

That means they have the better part of four years – not four weeks – to make one of the biggest financial decisions of their lives.

To assist the students and parents, we hire an expert, Dave Murray, to give them straight talk and helpful tips. Murray is the president of the National Center for College Costs, an organization that advises families about financial aid and the price of higher education.

Throughout the high school years, students and parents in our program can call Murray's staff with any question, whether it's about academics, campus social life or finances. Having access to that kind of an expert college consultant is something that is ordinarily available only to the affluent. We think working-class kids deserve the help. It's one important way to address the inequities in the college-bound journey.

A former dean of admissions at DePauw University in Indiana, Murray counsels students and parents of modest means about how much financial help colleges are likely to provide – and the extravagant sums that schools often expect working-class families to pony up.

Murray has witnessed a lot of very ugly war stories.

April is the toughest month, he said. *You pick up the phone, and it's a kid calling from the guidance office at the high school, and you can hear them crying.*

Almost everyone is familiar with the stories of disappointment experienced by a young person who has been rejected by a coveted college. But Murray also hears from a lot of heartsick students who were accepted by their dream schools.

These are students who received the big college packet in the mail with the congratulatory note. They whooped and hollered and did a victory lap. They called the grandparents with their good news. They donned the dream school tee shirt in the hallway parade at high school and excitedly texted friends about the cool campus they would soon be attending.

And then the rug was pulled out from under them.

They got into their dream school, he said. *But when the financial aid package arrives, it just doesn't work. There simply isn't enough money. And they are absolutely devastated.*

It's times like that when Murray draws on his master's degree in counseling.

You do a lot of hand-holding, sometimes literally, he said. *I have to build them back up emotionally. I tell them, 'You're going to be all right… no matter where you go to school. You're way too talented not to succeed in life.'*

And then he gently begins to explore some of the alternatives they might consider to that expensive and suddenly out-of-reach dream school.

We try to eliminate those eleventh-hour dramas by starting the college decision process at the beginning of high school, rather than near the end of it. The parents of freshman students in our partner high schools complete a form known as the College Cost Calculator. This is a formula that estimates the costs and aid they might expect from various colleges.

Wading through the financial aid bureaucracy can be intimidating, even maddening, especially if it's the first child in a family planning to attend college, or if the parents struggle with English. We walk the families through the process.

Murray visits our partner high schools and delivers a sixty-minute PowerPoint presentation that explores the issues that families should consider and the steps they need to take.

He explains that all students will eventually need to fill out the Free Application for Federal Student Aid form, commonly known as the FAFSA. The information on this application is used by the federal government to determine whether a student is eligible for a Pell Grant, a subsidy of up to $5,815 (for the 2016–17 school year) to those whose household income was under a certain threshold.

Eligibility depends on several factors, such as family income, the number of students in the home and how many kids are attending college. To be considered for our foundation's scholarship, a student must be eligible for a Pell Grant. Families are typically eligible for Pell if they earn less than $50,000, although most of the aid goes to families with income less than $20,000. We use Pell Grant eligibility as a definition of being a working-class student whose family is unlikely to have a lot of cash squirreled away for college.

The FAFSA counts the earnings of both parents, as long as they live together. Otherwise, it counts the income of the parent with whom the child lives a majority of the time. If the at-home parent is married to another person, it will also ask for the income of the stepparent. In calculating financial aid, the FAFSA does not count untaxed Social Security payments, the value of a home or money in a retirement account.

Besides determining whether a student is eligible for a Pell Grant, the information on FAFSA is used by a college itself to decide how much financial aid it will be willing to give to a particular student. This is known as institutional aid, since it is given to students at the discretion of the particular institution of higher education. The grant can vary widely from college to college, since some schools have very small endowments and others have very deep pockets.

Harvard, for example, has an endowment of more than $35 billion, the largest of any college in the world. That is why going to Harvard, and many other prestigious private schools, can often be less expensive than going to a local public school.

Other factors that come into play include the enrollment of the school, the number of other similar students with financial need, the school's appetite for first-generation, lower-income students and the policies of the governing bodies at the schools.

Colleges frequently boast about student bodies that are extremely diverse in terms of race, ethnicity, religion and nationality. But at many colleges, working-class students are notoriously underrepresented.

At Dartmouth College, a highly selective school in New Hampshire, 60 percent of the student body come from households in the top 6 percent of the national income distribution, those earning at least $200,000 a year, according to a 2015 report in the *Washington Post* by Craig Sutton, an associate professor of mathematics at the school. Only 11 percent of students, meanwhile, come from households in the bottom 40 percent of income, those earning less than $50,000. In other words, for every six Dartmouth students from the wealthiest US homes, there is only one student from the lower-middle class or below.

The conventional wisdom holds that rich families, given the advantages of wealth, simply produce many more capable scholars than do working-class people. But as Sutton notes, the gap in academic prowess between the economic classes is *not nearly as wide* as the gap in opportunity.

He pointed to a study by Caroline Hoxby, the Stanford economist, and Christopher Avery, of the Kennedy School at Harvard, which examined the economic backgrounds of top high school academic achievers. To qualify in this upper echelon, students needed at least an A-minus grade point average and an SAT or ACT score at the 90th percentile or above. The study found that households in the top 25 percent of income distribution accounted for 34 percent of high achievers, whereas the bottom quartile of households accounted for 17 percent of the high achievers.

In other words, Sutton explained, *for every two high-achieving students from the top quartile of the income distribution, we should expect one achiever from the bottom.*

That is not happening.

Too few working-class students apply to colleges in the first place, even among the very bright.

In the Give Something Back scholarship program, we encourage guidance counselors to make special efforts to reach out to those smart, lower-income students. The presence of a mentor helps students be aware that they are academically up to snuff in competing with more affluent students applying to colleges. Finally, building an active community of scholarship winners helps remind young students that others who share their socioeconomic status – whether it's an alum, a kid in the class before them, or even me – that others with challenges have successfully found a path to a college campus.

One of the deterrents to exploring college options among working-class kids and their parents, according to Murray, is that they are put off by the stated cost of attending a particular college.

As Murray explains to the families, students should never limit a college search by the advertised cost of tuition, room and board.

Almost nobody pays sticker price, he explains.

Stanford, as an example, is a very expensive school, but it has adopted a policy of charging zero tuition to students from families with an estimated gross income of $125,000 or less. Some of the wealthiest schools distribute financial aid even to families with incomes of $250,000.

In addition to requiring the FAFSA, some colleges will also require students to fill out a form known as the CSS/Profile. This form requires some information that is not measured by the FAFSA, such as home value, retirement accounts and the income of a parent who is not living with the child. Some colleges use the CSS/Profile to further refine its financial aid calculation.

Colleges also award merit scholarships that are not restricted by household income. Students with top grades or test scores, or those with special athletic or musical talent, as examples, are often awarded more generous financial aid packages.

Knowing these things as freshmen helps students better understand the importance of working hard in the classroom and developing special talents throughout the high school years. There is money at stake – sometimes enough to make the difference in whether it is possible to afford to attend a certain university.

If a student is considering a school that is far from home, it is important to add travel costs to the mix. The cost of textbooks, too, adds to the financial burden. The University of Illinois estimates that its annual cost of books typically exceeds $1,000.

When the financial aid package arrives, it includes the cost of tuition, housing and fees, the offer of grants (which do not have to be repaid), loans (which most certainly need to be repaid) and possibly a job on campus, sometimes known as Work Study.

The form will include the family's Expected Family Contribution, known as the EFC. That is the amount that a college believes the family can reasonably afford to pay toward the school bills. But that sum might not be enough to cover the difference between cost and aid.

The school is *gapping* the student – that is, leaving a gap between the cost and all of the combined resources: government grants, loans, institutional aid and a family's realistic contribution.

In effect, they might be saying: *You can't realistically afford to come here. We don't know how you're going to find the money. But if somehow you can scrape the loot together by begging or borrowing, then you are welcome to join us.*

Here's an example of what an offer might look like:

Costs		Financial Aid	
Tuition:	$22,000	Grants:	$10,000
Fees:	$2,000	Work Study:	$2,000
Housing:	$13,000	Loans:	$20,000

Expected Family Contribution: $5,000

At a quick glance, it might appear that the college is saying that the family's portion of the bill comes to $5,000. But if you look more closely, it tells a very different story. The family is actually on the hook for $27,000, as the $20,000 in loans must be repaid and the $2,000 in Work Study must be earned, requiring time spent that precludes other employment opportunities. Only the $10,000 in grant money is pure financial aid.

Murray's presentation helps families decipher the financial aid forms, and teaches them how they can make side-by-side comparisons of projected costs and financial aid offers at two or three colleges. That helps them become better education consumers, and it underscores the importance of preparation.

We don't want students to be ambushed as seniors, and we don't want them to rush in to making foolish choices. And we want to avoid those tearful telephone calls that Murray receives every April from crestfallen students who are unable to afford their dream school.

Of course, nothing is foolproof. Steve Cardamone, the executive director of the Give Something Back Foundation in Illinois, recounted a conversation with a student who was considering her college options.

She was admitted to two private universities in the Midwest of equivalent academic standing. College A made a virtual all-expenses-paid offer. College B required her to take on $19,000 in loans per year.

Cardamone typed the options side by side on a piece of paper. Then he folded the paper to show only College A, the school that was offering her a full ride. He pointed at that college and said in a firm tone, *That's the school you want.*

She unfolded the piece of paper and pointed at College B, the absurdly more expensive option.

But that's the school I want, she said.

She was seemingly oblivious to the huge debt. Down the road, when the bills start to arrive, she will have more clarity. By then, however, she will find herself in a deep hole.

In Murray's presentation, as well as in meetings with students and parents, he talks plainly about the real-life consequences of making extravagant choices to pay for college.

Parents take out whopping second mortgages, essentially forfeiting home equity that might have taken decades to build. That was a gambit that proved especially disastrous for families who took out a home loan at the fevered peak of property values in the late 2000s and then saw the value of their homes take a nosedive during the housing collapse.

Or they raid retirement savings that are going to be sorely needed someday – and a lot sooner than it might seem. In many cases, the parents co-sign for the students, and then supplement them with PLUS loans available to parents.

Murray too often sees students making choices that will tie them to heavy debt for decades.

To an eighteen-year-old student, the numbers might seem abstract and theoretical. Murray tries to make it seem a lot more real. He pulls out loan repayment schedules and plops them on a desk for a student to see in black and white.

And then he encourages them to imagine the future.

Is this really how you want to saddle yourself? You won't be able to afford to buy a home. It will be hard to afford a car. You won't be able to go on vacation.

Murray has been counseling students and families about college costs for a long time. He has watched the college debt crisis spread like wildfire.

I never had to have these conversations fifteen years ago, he explained. *It used to be, the costs were so much lower. And sure, there might be a student loan. But it was manageable. You'd look at the number and you could almost always figure out a way to make it work.*

As an example of how times have changed, a Pell Grant in 1980 covered about *three-quarters* of the cost of a four-year education at a public university.

Today it covers about *one-third*.

CHAPTER SEVEN

THE LAND OF PRIVILEGE AND POVERTY

The industrial city of Trenton, New Jersey, among countless factory towns across the nation, once provided manual jobs that offered a taste of middle-class life in a trade for sweat and brawn. This was a proud city with calloused hands that worked to feed the demand of distant markets.

Trenton Makes, the World Takes, as the local slogan put it.

Like so many other American factory towns, Trenton has never recovered from a manufacturing downturn that goes back to the 1970s. As in New Jersey's other industrial bases, like Newark and Camden, a majority of people in Trenton now live in poverty.

It is another tale altogether in places that rely on technology and information-based services, like the genteel town of Princeton. Its glistening boutiques are filled with stylish men, women and doted-upon children who look as if they have just stepped out of the pages of a very upscale catalog.

It is the land of plenty. Some of the most privileged children in town attend Princeton Day School, a private and highly selective academic institution that educates young people from pre-kindergarten through high school. It is a resplendent brick campus on Great Road in this town best known for its eponymous Ivy League school, a physicist named Albert Einstein and the twenty-fourth and twenty-eighth presidents of the United States, Grover Cleveland and Woodrow Wilson.

Students at Princeton Day go on class trips to China and Europe. The school has an architectural studio, six fields for lacrosse and field hockey, outdoor and indoor amphitheaters and a wonderful music facility. It has an ice rink and a figure skating team – *a figure skating team.* That pretty much sums it up.

For those who grow up with money and highly educated parents, kids take for granted from a very early age that they will go to college (give or take a rebellious streak along the way). As Robert Putnam notes in *Our Kids*, research shows that young people from the top quarter of families in education and income were *seventeen times more likely* to attend a highly selective college than were kids in the bottom quarter.

The tracking of kids begins long before they ever walk into a classroom. Studies show that an affluent child, by age three, has heard twenty million more words spoken in the home than a poor child has heard.

The differences continue practically nonstop throughout childhood, with rich kids far more likely to receive tutoring, take part in extracurricular activities, be exposed to the arts, or travel to other cities and countries.

Low-income children are far more likely to be born outside of marriage or to experience the divorce of parents. That usually means that kids spend less time with each parent, and have less money for books, sports and other enriching activities, since resources need to be spread to more than one household.

For single parents consumed with surviving from paycheck to paycheck, and battling the everyday stresses of child-rearing, there is a lot less time and energy left for plotting and executing the complicated (and sometimes absurdly competitive) journey from preschool to college.

As Charles Murray observed in his book, *Coming Apart: The State of White America*, a treatise on the growing class divide in America, *Eighteen-year-olds do not end up at Duke or Yale by accident…. They have already been socialized into the tastes and preferences of the upper-middle class, with little experience of any other realm of American life.*

When my children were young, I was not familiar with Princeton Day School. We were living in Florida, and we were concerned about our son, Ryan, who was struggling socially and performing poorly in the classroom.

It turns out he did not lack for academic talent. He was simply bored.

To my startled delight, standardized tests revealed that Ryan had registered test scores that were among the highest in the history of the school district. School officials told us he would be better off at a place that could more strongly challenge him intellectually.

At the time, I was considering going back to school myself and working on a doctoral degree. I like college towns. I wanted to live in an atmosphere with high energy, a community filled with open-minded people, and easy access to a diverse urban center. It was a scenario far-flung from my rural roots, which no doubt made the notion of a scholarly environment all the more appealing.

I did a serious search. I toured about fifty college towns. I considered Cambridge, home of Harvard and MIT. I visited Philadelphia, famous for the Liberty Bell, old money Main Line suburbs and Penn, the Ivy League college, as well as Villanova and Temple and LaSalle and St. Joseph's. I inspected Charlottesville, Virginia, home to presidents Thomas Jefferson and James Monroe, as well as the esteemed University of Virginia, where, at the time of my visit, an undergraduate named Tina Fey was majoring in drama (and surely, like other aspiring thespians, she was busy responding to the insistent question, *but how will you support yourself?*). And I went to Missouri, the state of my birth, where the first public institution of higher learning west of the Mississippi River was established in Columbia, a place that claims to have given birth to the autumn ritual of Homecoming.

But when I visited Princeton University, it felt magical. After a meeting with an official at the school – who encouraged me to apply for a doctoral candidacy – I walked along Nassau Street in search of a pay phone to call my wife, Jill.

We're moving to Princeton! I announced triumphantly.

In the end, I did not return to the classroom. What was more important: Ryan had been accepted to the very prestigious and very pricey Princeton Day School.

When we moved to New Jersey, Ryan was entering the fifth grade. At the time, it was a challenge for us financially.

It would turn out to be worth every penny.

Ryan blossomed. He eventually graduated as one of the top students in his class. He went off to Haverford College, and later moved to New York City, where he worked for a time at the *Paris Review*. He ended up earning a PhD at Yale in nineteenth-century American literature.

My daughter, Kelly, enrolled at Princeton Day in the third grade, and went on to serve on the Teen Council. She earned acceptance to Skidmore College, and then went through law school at the University of New Hampshire. My youngest child, Emmalee, attended Princeton Day through eighth grade and then decided to make a big switch: She chose to attend the Putney School, a progressive boarding school with a working dairy farm in Putney, Vermont. In making a switch from Princeton Day School, she had grown weary of the culture of materialism. She ultimately entered University of Miami.

PDS, as it is known locally, is an academic powerhouse. But it didn't score quite so well on socioeconomic diversity. The school was overwhelmingly white and wealthy, and the materialistic vibe of the place was impossible to ignore. The tuition tab alone for this day school, from pre-kindergarten through 12th grade, exceeds $350,000.

My children had wonderful educations at the school, but they lamented that the composition of the student body didn't exactly *look like America*, as they put it mildly. The rarefied atmosphere needed some down-to-earth perspectives.

That was something that hit close to home. When I started high school in Lockport, I owned a single pair of trousers and three shirts that had been handed down from my older brother.

Getting by without much, it turned out, was useful practice for much of my career in business. As an entrepreneur, I struggled for decades, until my fortunes soared in 2001. In the first big deal after the terror attack of 9/11, Wall Street investors wrote a check for $40 million for half-interest of my business. When we signed the deal in a Manhattan office, I remember scanning the room.

There were graduates of Harvard, Penn, Princeton, Stanford – and me – a product of a proud midwestern public school, the University of Illinois.

The company, Heartland Payment Systems, processed debit and credit transactions. When a card was swiped, Heartland would electronically link the customer, the business, the bank and the card brand, such as Visa or MasterCard, almost instantaneously.

From a start of 25 employees, Heartland grew to a workforce of more than 4,600. The company was worth $2 million when it was founded in 1997. In April of 2016, Heartland was sold for $4.3 billion.

To put that into perspective, consider that an investment of $1,000 made in March of 1997 – nineteen years and one month later – was worth $2,150,000.

In 2005, Heartland had gone public. We were living in the refurbished Tudor-style home of President Woodrow Wilson, primarily designed by his wife, Ellen, and constructed when he was a professor at Princeton.

Not so long before, I had to scrounge to find the money to pay the monthly tuition bill. Now the officials at the school were approaching me. I had become a member of the board of trustees at Princeton Day. And the school officials were asking for a big contribution for a capital campaign.

I asked how much.

They requested half a million bucks.

That's a lot of money, I replied.

I told them I'd think about it. So I went to my kids for advice.

My children urged me to fund scholarships for poor and working-class kids who could benefit from the chance to attend

Princeton Day, and whose perspectives and experiences would open the eyes of some of the privileged kids.

Up until then, Princeton Day had a relatively small number of students on scholarship. There were few students of color, and like their white classmates, they tended to come from privileged homes.

When I met with the leader of the project, I said I wasn't interested in contributing for a building. I certainly didn't want my name on any wall.

I was willing to make a contribution, however, based on certain stipulations.

The money would have to be used for scholarships for economically challenged students – kids of any color – who would otherwise have had no possible way to afford Princeton Day.

If the school agreed to those terms, I would give twenty times the amount requested – not $500,000, but a sum of $10 million.

One school administrator later said her jaw fell when she learned about the size of the offer. The school officials invited me to address a group of 150 faculty members and others on the school staff – everyone who helped play a part in nurturing an educational home for the Princeton Day students, from the principal to the custodians.

When I addressed the gathering, I thanked them for doing such important work. People in education don't hear that enough. Good teachers have a lot of heart and mighty intellectual horsepower. They are professionals who have watched peers, certainly not any smarter than they, choose career options that translated to a whole lot bigger paycheck and lives that appeared to be more glamorous.

I told these educators how they had changed the lives of so many children, including my own kids. I wanted them to have the chance to change even more lives.

I shared the experience of my son, Ryan, who had benefited so much at Princeton Day. When he had been in Florida, he didn't seem to find his place. He didn't share the same interests as the other boys. He didn't take to sports or racing.

Instead, he read voraciously. At Princeton Day, for the first time, he was in a place where his peers valued him for his intellect. It changed the way he looked in the mirror. Shortly after Ryan enrolled at the school, he told me that he felt like he had finally *come home.*

As I told the story to the school staff, I choked up. Before my talk was over, I think everyone in the room was tearful.

It made all of us feel more precious, said Judy Fox, the head of school. *It made us all sit just a little bit taller in our chairs.*

It was Princeton Day that showed me the importance of connecting with kids early in their lives, focusing on their talents and lighting a fire, rather than waiting until they were nearly done with high school. The revelation would change my approach to giving scholarships back in Illinois.

I was informed that my gift would be the largest donation ever to a nonresidential school. I did some investigating. I learned that Bill Gates had also made a $10 million donation to his boyhood school. In at least this one category, I was tied with the famous software genius.

I saw his contribution – and I raised mine.

Let's make it $11 million, I told the school officials.

So my contribution became the largest ever to a nonresidential K-12 school.

We needed to get the word out that a new day had arrived for Princeton Day. The doors were going to swing open to more kids with scarce resources. To market the program, we visited some churches and community groups in poorer sections of the region.

Among people struggling to get by, there was only a passing familiarity with Princeton Day. To people in hardscrabble neighborhoods, the school was correctly viewed as an extremely prestigious prep school for the very smart and the very privileged.

The school wasn't so many miles away from them, but for practical purposes, it might as well have been on Mars.

Now it was within reach.

These were people who had walked a tough road in life, and were courageously stepping up to do whatever was possible for kids they loved. Many were single parents. There were a lot of grandmas raising children, and aunts and uncles, too.

A lot of them were people who could have taken an easier route, but who stepped up to protect a child. You could hear that protectiveness in their questions.

They were understandably skeptical of this white corporate executive coming to talk about a free education for their children at a fancy school.

'What's in this for you?'

'Why are you doing this?'

'What's your motive?'

My answers were simple. My company had been successful beyond my wildest dreams. I wanted to give back to help some hardworking kids who deserved a break.

As it turned out, we wouldn't need to do a lot of marketing. When talk of the scholarships got around, articles appeared in newspapers in Trenton and Princeton. School counselors quickly got wind of it, and before we knew it, the school was being flooded with calls.

Princeton Day was intent on protecting the privacy of the kids in the scholarship program. They didn't want them to be labeled as *the poor kids*. And some of the faculty members expressed concerns about whether the new students would have some difficulty in acclimating to the new culture.

They didn't need to worry. From the first day, some of our younger scholarship kids walked down the halls of the school and identified themselves by proudly proclaiming: *I'm a Give Something Back scholar!*

These kids would more than fit in – they would become leaders at Princeton Day School.

Dominique Samuels was growing up without some things other kids took for granted. She and her mother lived at her grandma's in a modest home in a struggling section of Trenton. Her mom worked for the Department of Motor Vehicles and did the best she could. Her dad, meanwhile, had never been a part of her life. Money was scarce.

What Dominique did not lack was brilliance. By the time she reached the fourth grade at her school in Trenton, it had become clear that she was not being sufficiently challenged academically.

When she started at Princeton Day as a fifth grader, her new peers challenged her – and she had the smarts to challenge them, too.

She noticed some differences as soon as she entered the affluent school. It was very preppy, a lot of polo shirts and khakis.

She noticed the kids displayed certain mannerisms, which she chalked up to an aristocratic upbringing.

Some of the phrases and expressions didn't sound like the talk back in her old neighborhood. After winter and spring breaks, plenty of the kids would come back and talk about trips to faraway, exotic places.

Dominique did not feel threatened or insecure. This was a kid with moxie.

I always knew I didn't have as much money, but it didn't affect me, she said. *I knew my mom worked just as hard as theirs did, and maybe harder. So I never felt like they were better.*

She found a passion for social activism. She joined the Black and Latino Student Union. And she helped found a group for those of all backgrounds interested in fostering unity and understanding. It was called Student Association for Everyone. The organization had a tall task, but a simple premise.

At the end of the day, said Dominique, *we're all the same.*

She never lost sight that students at Princeton Day had opportunities not available to kids at other schools. In anatomy class, she and others were taken to a medical center to watch a surgery. For another class, she visited an appellate court and met with a judge.

Most of her classmates did not have jobs, other than perhaps helping out at an expensive summer camp. Dominique worked at a pizza place and taught ballet at the YMCA.

In her high school years, she took advantage of the school's resources, making frequent visits to college counselors and spending a long time talking about her options.

The girl who lived next door, Dominique recalled, *was really proud of what I was doing.*

In her senior year, she was accepted to Davidson College, among the most competitive liberal arts schools in the nation.

With the heavy workload at Davidson, and the high expectations, she often studied past midnight, pushing as hard as she could and reminding herself that she could meet and exceed the limits of whatever she imagined possible.

It was a spirit that inspired Dominique's classmates, kids with more smarts than money, like Dennis Cannon.

After Dennis's parents divorced, he lived in a rough-at-the-edges apartment complex with his mom, Tara. When he entered Princeton Day on a scholarship, he remembered thinking: *These kids wear some really nice clothes. And man, the classes are tough!*

In his sophomore year, Dennis was elected vice president of his class. As a junior, he was captain of the football team. As a senior, he was captain of the baseball team.

He became president of the Athletic Association, which promoted school spirit. He joined an organization called Youth for the Elderly, which spent hours every Sunday visiting the lonely residents of homes for the aged in the Princeton area.

An athlete with a big dose of charisma and kindness, Dennis would have fit in at any school. In a quiet way, he became a mentor to the scholarship students who came after him.

The thing we had in common was financial instability, he recalled, *and that was something the upper-class kids couldn't understand.*

Riding the school bus, as some of the scholarship kids did, was hard to fathom for the privileged kids.

'*Why won't your mom drive you?*'

'*Or your nanny?*'

Dennis went out of his way to give a boost to any scholarship kid who seemed to be experiencing doubts about being worthy.

One was a kid who rose before dawn to catch her bus, and fought to maintain her energy through the day. She confided to Dennis about her worries. She wasn't sure she had the talent to succeed at Princeton Day School.

He gave her a pep talk.

You already have succeeded, he told her. *You get up at 5 a.m. to catch a bus! You use your strength to fight your way through. And you are smart. Don't doubt that.*

The network of scholarship kids looked out for one another. Some called their group *the posse.* They knew the importance of giving back.

In the high school yearbook at fancy Princeton Day, a kid from gritty Trenton, Alejandra Arrué, was named Student Most Likely to Succeed.

Alejandra never considered herself poor. She didn't have a car, a perk that was taken for granted by some other high school kids at Princeton Day School. When she needed to find quiet to study in her family's small home, she often retreated to a closet. And her father had gone through a rough period with his work. But she made clear that she was not living in poverty.

I had clothes, she said, *and I had enough to eat.*

In fact, Alejandra talked mostly about the help she received at Princeton Day with college prep, working on the Common Application essay as early as her sophomore year.

I've had a privileged life, she said, *regardless of my parents' income.*

Alejandra has made the most of it. She attended prestigious Barnard College in New York. She also remembered the importance of paying back. She worked for Teach for America at a poor, largely immigrant school in Texas. She also pays back her student loans, about $500 a month.

Her balance grew to nearly $50,000. She knew other grads owed a lot more. But it still weighed on her.

I pay the loan bill every month, she said, *and the total doesn't seem to go down.*

At age five, Mark Washington was diagnosed with Crohn's disease, a serious digestive condition. The boy would regularly miss school for hospitalizations after flare-ups. It took eight months for doctors to correctly pinpoint the problem. The poor kid was miserable.

Living with Crohn's disease got in the way of his life. As he proceeded through second grade, he fell behind in his schoolwork. He had also become very quiet, even withdrawn, a reaction that is not uncommon for young children who have gone through such painful trauma.

His mom, Myra Washington, was concerned about her son lagging so far behind. A friend suggested that he apply for a slot at Princeton Day.

He's such a bright boy, the friend said. *They'll push him along so he can catch up.*

Myra Washington knew the school was very selective. She hesitated about even giving it a shot, but finally urged Mark to give it a try. As part of the application, Mark took standardized tests. He sat with other kids and took part in a class. He had one-on-one interviews with the faculty.

His mom grew discouraged about his chances. She will never forget the day the letter from Princeton Day came in the mail.

She was on her way out the door, en route to the grocery store, when she picked up the mail and saw the Princeton Day School envelope. She was too nervous to open it.

She drove to the store, parked the car and held the envelope in her trembling hands.

I was so scared, she said. *I held it and I prayed.*

When she opened it, she read that Mark had been accepted and was being awarded a full scholarship.

I cried and cried, said Myra.

And then she called her husband, Mark Washington Sr. He let out a thundering cheer.

It was a very happy day, she said.

Mark was in third grade when he entered Princeton Day. Soon he experienced a serious recurrence of his symptoms. He was hospitalized for seven days at the Children's Hospital of Philadelphia.

His teacher, Betsy Rizza, would call Mark in the hospital to comfort him and go over his school lessons. The school made special arrangements to insure that Mark would not fall behind academically.

In the high school level, Mark's disease became more manageable. He played guard on the school basketball team. He wore number 23. His parents noticed he started to smile a lot more than before.

No place is perfect. Like some other black and Latino kids, or those of any color who know the meaning of economic struggle, navigating a way among the privileged can be difficult, even hurtful.

They don't always understand that they live in a certain world, said Mark, noting that the wealthy kids *wear a different outfit every day* to school.

Some of the kids make remarks that sting. There was the time when a black girl was passing by, and one of the wealthy white kids muttered *illiterate* under his breath.

That's what they think of us, he told his mother. *They think black people are illiterate and that everyone in Trenton carries guns.*

When things got to Mark, he sought out Gil Olvera, who oversaw the scholars in the Give Something Back Foundation.

When something goes wrong, when there's bullying – or a comment about race or ethnicity, Olvera said, *I seek them out.*

As he put it: *My job is to listen. I tell them that I've gone through some similar things and it's turned out okay.*

Growing up deprived can limit your range of experiences and perspectives. But so can growing up wealthy in a kind of golden cocoon.

At Princeton Day, Olvera recalled a young Latina student walking into a room and hearing some wealthy white boys call out, '*Hey, Esmeralda!*' Her name was not Esmeralda. And then the wealthy boys made a wiping motion as if they were beckoning her to clean their table.

The rich kids had grown up accustomed to the notion that it was the role of brown people to serve and wait on people like them. They thought they were being amusing. The Latina did not take it that way.

To lend support to students of color and whites facing economic challenges, Olvera conducted assemblies at the school, with guest speakers who addressed issues of race and class.

Carly Ozarowski, an affluent white girl, said her education would have been a lot poorer without the perspectives of people from different backgrounds, to say nothing of her friendships.

You're reminded how lucky you are, said Carly, a former figure skating performer at Princeton Day School who went on to major in sociology at Connecticut College. *When I was little, I pretty much thought everyone had the advantages that I had. I learned differently.*

Each year, eighth graders delivered a speech to the entire middle school. It required skill, creativity – and a lot of guts.

When Fernando Erazo delivered his speech, some of his classmates said they were changed forever.

Fernando talked about the importance of struggle. As he explained, his biggest struggle was simply getting into the United States, which meant spending two months in a detention center in Texas.

Our group would walk at night, so the helicopters and airplanes passing overhead wouldn't see us, he told his peers.

The nights were cold. The days were blazing.

He was six years old, the only child traveling with a group of about ten adults, including his mother. When they crossed over the border into Texas, they were arrested.

We were taken to a family prison, he explained. *We spent two long months stuck in that place…. We had a small room with bunk beds, a single bathroom and a small, skinny rectangular window where we could barely see the sun.*

At the end of the incarceration, a judge permitted the boy and his mother to stay in the United States, with travel restrictions. Fernando was reunited with his father, who had left when his son was only two months old.

Fernando would need to learn the language, new customs and make a new home in a place called New Jersey. He had endured a long journey, spent two months in a family prison and left behind many friends and relatives.

But hey, look where I'm standing now, he said. *After going through all those hard times, I have started down the road to the American dream.*

He thanked his family, the staff at Princeton Day, and his coach, John.

I have to take all the chances I get… take risks, like the risk my mom took in coming to this country, he said. *I decided to tell you this story of my life because there will be times when you'll say, 'Why is this happening to me?'*

He stood before his classmates, many of whom had been given every opportunity and privilege as a birthright.

Open your eyes to the opportunities in this amazing country, he said. *And never take it for granted.*

Joshua Meekins, one of the scholarship students, has come back to work at the foundation and help more kids find opportunity.

A graduate of Villanova University, he works as a program coordinator, speaker and a young executive who finds mentors for our students. As an African American, Joshua knows the importance of being a kid of color who can look up to a mentor and relate to someone who looks like him or her and has achieved success.

When he was chosen for a scholarship to Princeton Day, he later confessed to a group of our Give Something Back students, he experienced what he described as survivor's remorse – a kid from a tough neighborhood who got a break – while so many others did not.

There were other students who were just as talented as I, yet I was chosen and they weren't, he said. *I felt a little guilty about it. Was I worth the investment? Could I measure up? Someone else believed in me, but could I believe in myself? I could. I did. And I stand here before all of you as a testament that this thing called life is not gonna work if you don't believe in yourself.*

CHAPTER EIGHT

ON THE FENCE

For kids like Noah, Nicole, Frances and Shannon – academic stars who went on to become a physician, a chemist, an executive and a lawyer – winning a scholarship was a wonderful accomplishment. They were thrilled to be chosen. They needed the money. And they remain grateful to this day.

But I didn't kid myself. These exceptionally bright and highly motivated students would have found a way to go to college, with or without the help of Bob Carr.

The money helped them graduate with much less debt. That counted for a lot. But they would have found a way to get into a good college and make their way to the commencement stage. When it came to achieving academic goals, these were kids who were not going to be stopped.

Students at the top of the class have a pick of colleges. Some of them gain admission to some of the most elite schools in the nation. One of our scholarship winners became perhaps the first student in the history of Lockport Township High School to attend Harvard.

I cheered loudly for these brilliant kids – and I still do.

But I wanted to make a real difference in the lives of kids who might not go to *any* college without help. We turned our focus to those young people with more modest hopes and tenuous circumstances, students who might go to college, or who would start college, take on crippling debt, and then drop out without a degree.

Swooping in with scholarships during the senior year of high school, I came to realize, was really showing up a bit late in the game. For a lot of working-class kids, the fork in the road comes in the middle school years. So our foundation in Illinois moved the scholarship program to a much younger group of students.

For a time, we were awarding the scholarships as early as the sixth grade. But organizing the program at so many elementary schools, with so many different administrators and counselors, proved unwieldy. For practical reasons, we ultimately settled on selecting scholarship winners during the freshman year of high school.

Moving the awards to a younger age allowed us to expand the reach of our influence. We weren't simply handing off a prize as a student walked out of the doors of high school. Instead, we were greeting them at the beginning of high school with a promise:

If you study hard, take college-prep courses, maintain a B average and keep your nose clean, you'll have a prepaid college scholarship waiting for you.

A lot has been written about the anxieties of upper-middle-class kids, and some brilliant working-class kids, too, who lay awake at night, worrying about gaining admission to one of the hallowed colleges on the top-ranked lists. But the difference between going to one of the glamour colleges, as opposed to enrolling in a more modest, but perfectly solid school, is not the life changer that some might imagine.

A much bigger difference can be measured between those who graduate from any college – and those who do not graduate.

The evidence for this was revealed in a study by Seth D. Zimmerman, an economist at the University of Chicago. He conducted a study that examined students who straddled either side of the admissions cutoff at less-selective colleges. Perfectly fine schools, not known as prestigious, these were colleges that served many working-class students.

He looked at those clustered on the margin, students with similar test scores and grades. Those *just above* the admission line, the economist found, would end up earning substantially more by their late twenties than did the students *just below* the admissions line – simply by virtue of the fact that they got a chance to go to college and earn a degree.

In practical terms, those in both groups were virtually equal in terms of smarts and capabilities. And yet, since those below the line didn't get in, the long-term consequences were economically significant.

Zimmerman contended that the results underscored a powerful reality for young people teetering on the college fence. What mattered most was not *where* you go, but *whether* you go.

If you give these students a shot, Zimmerman told the *New York Times*, *they're ready to succeed.*

We know that we are missing out on a lot of talent. This study and other research underscores the reality that millions of people have the ability to earn a bachelor's degree – but are not doing so.

To reach more underprivileged students, we expanded our scholarship program beyond Lockport, to all of those in surrounding Will County, as long as they qualified for a federal Pell Grant, usually an income of $50,000 or less. We would later grow to provide scholarships at the University of Illinois and Northern Illinois University. We ventured to other states, too, establishing partnerships with colleges in New Jersey, New York, Delaware and Pennsylvania, with plans to reach throughout the United States.

I have contributed more than $25 million to this cause. Some generous donors have joined our effort. We are intent on capitalizing on our investment. In other words, we want to significantly increase the number of kids we can help send to college and help graduate without debt.

We took an unusual approach: We decided we would try to strike a bargain with the colleges.

In seeking partner schools, we looked to solid institutions with reasonable admissions requirements – places that accepted students who didn't necessarily have perfect grades and test scores. In particular, these would be colleges with a demonstrated history of success in educating the working-class, first-generation students and immigrant families.

This was our offer: We would give $1 million to the school to invest however it wished – bank the money and collect interest, put it into a mutual fund that would yield growth, designate it for a capital campaign.

In exchange, the college would promise to grant full scholarships to fifty of our Give Something Back scholars – students who were then high school freshmen – when the time came for them to enroll in college.

Our kids would then apply for financial aid, and the federal and state grants they received would go toward the tuition and room and board bills. The college, meanwhile, would have our contributions and the interest income to use. But they would be required to guarantee admission at no cost for tuition and fees and room and board. If there were a gap between the aid and the sticker price, the school would need to cover the margin.

The agreement means the colleges give discounts to our students. But the schools also get a lot in return. We essentially have served as a recruitment and marketing arm for our partner colleges. Because we impose standards on grades, moreover, and demand high character of our scholars, we effectively serve as screeners, interviewers and mentors for the colleges.

Perfect high school grades aren't everything. As any employer will tell you, determination and character can count for more than almost anything else.

Chuck Beutel, vice president of admissions at one of our partner schools, the University of St. Francis in Illinois, said his college was grateful to be getting kids from poor and working-class backgrounds.

These were students, many of them first-generation Americans, who had never walked across a campus. They were smart, but perhaps every bit as important, they were kids who knew what it meant to hang tough in life. They did not suffer from being overprivileged.

These are kids who grew up knowing they had to work very hard for everything they've gotten, Beutel said. *And it shows.*

Businesses and other employers see the value of a college degree, in large part, as evidence that a person has committed to something and stuck with it successfully. Whether the major is in the humanities or the hard sciences, persistence and drive are qualities that will translate in the workplace.

Education experts have coined a word for those who have that kind of drive: grit. And almost every employer will tell you that grit can reveal more about future success than test scores or grades.

Our scholarship comes with strings. Our students need to take a college preparatory course load and demonstrate aptitude. They are expected to stay out of trouble. It's a motivational tool. When a student knows that big scholarship bucks are on the line, they have every reason to choose the right path.

Some kids stumble along the way, of course. People make mistakes, and younger people tend to make even more of them. We have been known to give a second chance to a young person, and even a third chance. In rare instances, however, students have been dropped from the program for failing to comply with standards. Life demands accountability, and we are doing students no favors if we pretend otherwise.

Indeed, lowering expectations for these students would not be a favor, but rather a concession to defeat. That can amount to a damaging form of discrimination. Michael Gerson, a former speechwriter for George W. Bush, described it as *the soft bigotry of low expectations.*

On the whole, of course, our program is much more carrot than stick. As one principal put it, when a kid fresh out of the eighth grade sees a full-ride scholarship on the table, *the world of possibility suddenly gets a lot bigger.*

Working-class and economically struggling students, whose families might have seen a university education as a perk reserved for the privileged, suddenly see a reason to dream – and hit the books.

CHAPTER NINE

GOOD GRADES AND COLD CASH

As a child, I had already settled on my professional occupation. I was going to play second base for the Chicago White Sox.

Somehow, it didn't turn out that way.

The ballparks and gymnasiums of America today are filled with kids and parents with dreams of athletic scholarships to college. Except for a minuscule percentage of them, of course, it just isn't going to happen.

Between 1 and 2 percent of college students are receiving athletic scholarships. And the chance of winning a full-ride athletic scholarship is microscopic. The average sports scholarship yields far less than the sum required to pay college bills.

There are all kinds of good reasons for young people to participate in sports, but looking at it as a strategy to pay for college is not one of them. Across all economic classes, parents who tell their young children they can win a sports scholarship – besides putting kids under a lot of pressure – are likely setting their kids up for failure without realizing it.

A far surer chance of winning college scholarship money lies in earning good grades and scoring well on admissions exams. But that path isn't talked about nearly as much.

Financial aid packages at most colleges are fattened by many thousands of dollars if an applicant has achieved good grades and scores. The Give Something Back Foundation, like other scholarship programs, gives great weight to the grades of our candidates.

Although few people think of it this way, a student who works to make good grades is already earning a lot of money in college savings, given the impact these marks have on college aid.

It starts early. Students who wait until junior or senior year of high school to get serious about college, unfortunately, have often put themselves behind the eight ball. High school transcripts and class rank include the grade for the very first course in the freshman year, and everything that comes afterwards.

Even before freshman year, it is important to earn good grades. Besides honing useful study habits and a healthy respect for learning, students who perform well in the sixth, seventh and eighth grades are more likely to be placed in Advanced Placement classes in high school. These classes not only count for college credit at many schools – a big savings – they enhance the resume of any applicant seeking money in merit scholarships.

Parents who spend a lot of time cheering the sports triumphs of their kids – and they should cheer for them – should also be applauding loudly when their young ones crack the books.

This is not simply an issue for economically disadvantaged families. Many people with incomes well above the Pell Grant level find themselves staggered by the breathtakingly high cost of college.

With top grades and a score of 33 on her ACT exam, Maddie Dwyer had put herself in a position to gain admission to some of the most prestigious colleges in America.

But just before the start of her senior year in high school, everything changed. Her dad suffered a devastating stroke that left him permanently disabled and unable to work.

A fancy college name, with a costly price tag, was not an option. Maddie would need to find a school willing to offer her a big scholarship.

Her mother, Darby Dwyer, steeped herself in research, surfing the Internet for schools around the country that offered sizable awards for students who meet certain academic criteria.

Maddie grew up in the upper Midwest, but she ultimately chose to enroll at the University of Mississippi. Ole Miss is one of many schools that offer fixed scholarships to students who have earned top grades and test scores.

By attending Mississippi, Maddie graduated with zero debt. She earned an undergraduate education without her or her parents spending a dime. At Mississippi, she was an academic standout in the honors program.

After graduation, she enrolled in Drexel University College of Medicine in Philadelphia.

Maddie's older brother, Jack, attended the University of Alabama on a scholarship. A younger brother, Kevin, achieved test scores that earned him a full ride to Mississippi.

The college decisions by the Dwyer children – and the research done by their mom – was cumulatively worth hundreds of thousands of dollars to the family.

Considering the money at stake and the long-term benefits of a college degree, it seems foolish to take out big loans without doing some homework about the potential options.

If you were going to spend $60,000 on a car, Darby noted, *you would certainly do some research before you bought it.*

Schools anxious to enhance their profiles in the *US News* ranking will bend over backwards – and award plenty of money – to attract students with top scores and good grades.

Mississippi posts the requirements for scholarships on its website, as do many other schools. There is no wondering and waiting for an offer from a financial aid office, and the subsequent rush to decide in the hectic eleventh hour whether a certain school is worth the price.

By learning what is available, and making the applications, students and parents can take plenty of time in choosing a school and avoid making a rash decision that might end up costing a fortune in student debt.

A website available through College Confidential offers pages and pages of scholarships around the country, along with eligibility requirements: http://talk.collegeconfidential.com/financial-aid-scholarships/1461983-competitive-full-tuition-full-ride-scholarships.html

It pays to get an early start on the college entrance exams, the ACT or SAT, perhaps in the middle or end of the sophomore year, rather than waiting until the spring of junior year.

By testing early, students can determine a baseline and work on improvement. Tutors can provide one-on-one help. Such tutoring might cost $1,000. That might seem like a lot of money, but higher scores can save that amount many times over.

It's almost never a good idea to fall in love with a dream school or even think in terms of a top choice. It can cloud judgment and court disappointment. Many schools can provide a great education, a lot of fun and preparation for a successful career.

Students should apply early. And they should apply to many schools. For families with lower incomes, many colleges waive the application fee.

There are many scholarships that go unclaimed every year. College scholarships are tailored for students of almost every background and circumstance. Awards are given to vegetarians, skateboarders and children of inmates, even for those who have found creative ways to use the Star Trek language of Klingon.

In her smart pursuit of an affordable college degree, Monika Dargis figured out a way to save both money and time.

Monika's dad was a police officer. Her mom worked as a school secretary. There wasn't a big pile of money stashed away for college. She decided it made sense for her to spend her first year going to a local community college – not just for the first academic year, but for the calendar year.

She explained her community college strategy: *I wanted to take as much as I could, as soon as I could, and get out as quickly as possible.*

Rather than wait for the fall semester to begin after high school graduation, she used the summer to take a full load at her local community college. She continued to take heavy academic loads – twenty hours in the fall semester and twenty hours in the spring semester. And then she enrolled in summer school once again.

Taking heavy loads and going to school year-round meant that Monika was able to earn two years of college credit in roughly a single year. By the time fall rolled around, she was able to enroll at the University of Wisconsin–Madison as a junior, even though her high school classmates – who had gone directly to a four-year university – were only starting their sophomore years. (Those who had fallen behind in credits, moreover, were still freshmen.) In effect, Monika was graduating from college in three years.

People would sometimes ask my age and my year at college, said Monika, *and they'd say, 'Wait, that doesn't add up!'*

Financially, it added up in a big way. She saved nearly $70,000 (two years of tuition and housing at Wisconsin) by living at home and going to community college for a single academic year, bookended with sessions of summer school. After earning her bachelor's degree in psychology, Monika went to graduate school with the help of grants, including an award from the National Mental Health Institute. She ultimately was accepted into the doctorate program at Madison.

As early as their ninth grade year, Cole Byram and many of his classmates were attending college without leaving the premises of Jennings County High School in rural Indiana.

In what is known as a *dual credit program*, Cole and many of his classmates enrolled as early as the ninth grade in classes that counted for both high school and college transcripts.

By the time Cole enrolled at Butler University in Indianapolis in 2015, just a few months after his high school commencement, he was already a member of the junior class.

It saved him a fortune in college costs. With tuition and housing costs running about $50,000 a year at Butler, Cole's head start translated to a savings of about $100,000.

It was a windfall for his working-class family. His dad was a retired union electrical contractor. His mom worked the books for the business.

My parents were thrilled, said Cole, *to say the least.*

Ivy Tech, the largest community college system in the country, designs and oversees courses for high school students to gain post-secondary credit. It is a sweet deal for high school students. They can take college courses for college credit without paying college tuition.

In the school year of 2014–15, more than fifty thousand Indiana high school students, most of them juniors and seniors, completed coursework that qualified for dual credit.

For Ivy Tech alone, that's $40 million of savings in college costs for students and families, said Dr. John Newby, an assistant vice president for the system headquartered in Indianapolis.

Other colleges in Indiana and throughout the country offer similar dual credit curricula. These programs provide another way for families to make college affordable to working-class students and families.

In the case of Ivy Tech, the college sets standards for the courses, which are taught by high school teachers. Many high school students use the classes for credits in technical fields, preparing for good-paying jobs in trades like welding or auto mechanics. Others take courses that count toward an associate's degrees required for careers in nursing, as an example.

Many other students, like Cole, use these courses to build transcripts at four-year colleges long before they set foot on campus. The dual credit classes at high schools are twice as long as the same classes in college. In other words, high school students spend two semesters on a class that would be completed in a single semester at college. The extra time helps ensure that high school students are able to master the more difficult, college-level material.

By state law, all Indiana colleges and universities must accept the dual credit on a student's transcript. Schools in other states accept or deny the Ivy Tech dual credit on a case-by-case basis.

The dual credit program was tailor-made for a smart, hardworking student like Cole. He earned dual credit in Advanced Placement courses such as physics, United States history, English literature, chemistry and government, among others. He was also president of the senior class and the National Honor Society. He belonged to the Spanish Club and was captain of the academic team.

He planned to major in accounting, but added *politics is my passion.* He hoped to run for elective office, starting with the school board and perhaps going all the way up to Congress.

After enrolling at Butler, he promptly ran for two elective offices. He lost a run for representative of his dorm, but won a bid for the student senate.

As soon as he graduated from college, he said, he planned to run for his local school board, and then climb the ladder *all the way up through federal offices.*

Graduating ahead of the great majority of his peers, Cole would have an early start to pursue his dreams, and he would have some extra money in his pocket.

CHAPTER TEN

MENTORS MAKE THE DIFFERENCE

From a very early age, I remember hearing my parents mock college professors and students.

As my father saw it, college was full of pointy-headed intellectuals, effete snobs with affected airs who lacked common sense.

In my working-class family, nobody had gone to college. People who went on to higher education, I was brought up to believe, were our social enemies. The same was true of people in the business world. They were successful simply because they had stolen from humble and hardworking people like us.

My dad, Arthur Charles Carr, worked a blue-collar job at Argonne National Laboratory and, towards the end, he said that he hated it. My mother worked nights as a waitress. She came home at night with feet so sore she soaked them in Epsom salts. My parents chafed at their places in life, but they held an even deeper mistrust for those who wanted to climb any career ladders.

Looking back, it's easy to see that a lot of the talk, especially from my dad, masked a deep sense of insecurity.

If you go to college, you'll look down on people like us!

He insisted that I consider a career in the military.

The army will make a man out of you!

And that was something he thought would do me good. He had called me a sissy many times, once when I was thirteen years old, after church on Easter Sunday, while he was slapping me around – again and again – for humiliating him by singing in a choir with girls.

Like choir, college was apparently a place for sissies.

When you're a kid, it can be difficult to separate the truth from nonsense. That's why good mentors are so important for students, especially for those of us who come from families who see college as an alien world.

When I was in the seventh grade, I had a social studies teacher named Bob Langlois. He was also the coach of our baseball squad.

Mr. Langlois had been a minor league baseball player. In the eyes of a sports-crazy boy in the seventh grade like me, being a pro ball player – even if you didn't make it to the big leagues – meant that you had walked in the land of heroes.

Despite my dreams of playing for my beloved Chicago White Sox, I was not destined for pro ball. Coach Langlois understood the limits of my baseball talents. He put me in right field. I played on the third string. In my hardball career, I batted twice and struck out both times. As a softball player, I was a star. But my baseball aspirations ended in the eighth grade.

Beyond baseball, Coach Langlois recognized that I was a smart kid. Every day during social studies, he would pick a word from the dictionary and ask for a volunteer to give the definition. He also quizzed us about state capitals. I raised my hand so many times he finally pulled me aside and politely suggested that I give some other kids a chance.

When I mentioned to Mr. Langlois that I wouldn't be going to college, he corrected me as swiftly and directly as if I had just given the wrong answer to a definition or swung and missed on a state capital.

You are going to college!

To me, Mr. Langlois was like God.

And so I told him: *If you think I can, I'll do it.*

You are going to college, he repeated.

When I left home to attend the University of Illinois, I had never set foot on a college campus.

The day I headed for college, I stepped on the train in the Chicago south suburb of Homewood, alone but knowing that my life would finally be changing, a change that I had eagerly been awaiting for several years. At the age of seventeen, I felt like I had finished my sentence and finally been released by the warden, my father, and was free at last.

The old Illinois Central rolled through the gone-in-a-blink little towns and vast farm fields before finally pulling into Champaign. It seemed to me like a long-awaited and joyous journey to a faraway land. In important ways, that's what it was for me. And change my life it did.

I grabbed my luggage and went searching for the building where I would pick up my Air Force uniform. In those days, all male underclassmen at the University of Illinois were required to serve in the ROTC.

In my years at Illinois, my parents never came to visit me, not even for the commencement ceremony where I received my master's degree diploma at age twenty-one.

College changed the way I pictured myself and the way I saw the world. I was lucky to have had Bob Langlois in my life.

Mr. Langlois later left the teaching and coaching ranks and went into business on his own. For a couple of summers after high school, I worked for him. Years down the road, when I was running my own computer consulting business, I hired him to work for me for a time.

My experience with Mr. Langlois taught me about the power of mentors. For kids of any circumstance, it helps to have a booster. It is especially important for students whose parents are absent, overwhelmed or unfamiliar with the college process.

When I talk to educators – whether they teach at an elementary school or serve as the president of a large university – they invariably cite mentoring as one of the most important tools for academic and emotional success.

Teenagers might look like young adults, but they're still just kids. And even though they might protest about rules or restrictions, research shows that kids want more structure in their lives. For all the eye rolling, they want someone to be watching.

Unfortunately, they are often wandering alone. Teenagers spend a vast majority of the time outside school without any companionship or supervision, according to a 2013 study funded by the Gates Foundation. And it makes a difference when a mentor steps into the picture.

Young people who regularly meet with a mentor are 46 percent less likely to use drugs and 27 percent less likely to drink, according to the Gates study, and they are less apt to suffer from depression.

Other studies have found that mentoring translates to better grades and attendance records and fewer problems with bullying.

For kids whose parents did not go beyond high school, mentors who can talk about college provide an essential bridge.

At the Give Something Back Foundation, each of our high school scholarship kids is paired with a mentor. It is not complicated. Having a degree in social work or psychology is not a requisite. What is required is the commitment to caring, listening, encouraging and being available.

Becky Paaso, one of our mentors, routinely sends a message to her young charges that sums it up:

I'm here.

Our mentors communicate with the students at least once every couple of weeks – in person, on the phone, or by email, text or Skype. The mentors drop in at school to watch a student play in a ballgame (or ride the bench), perform in a theater production or a concert. The mentors arrange for the kids to shadow someone who is working in a particular career field that interests the student. They look for signs of trouble and temptation, and talk a lot about priorities and the wonderful possibilities that await them.

The mentors become familiar with school schedules and know when a test is on the horizon. They remind a student to be prepared – and they often step in themselves as tutors.

But it is not all about schoolwork. In every school in the land, some students walk the hallways and feel invisible. Others feel pressures at home, especially when a parent is absent or anxious or ill.

In Natalie Rigoni's sophomore year of high school, the world seemed to be falling apart. Her parents had divorced. Her father's small construction business was struggling to survive a housing downturn – and then her dad was diagnosed with cancer.

Natalie, who lived with her dad and her three brothers, *sort of took over the role of the mom in the house.*

The leaders of our foundation in Illinois – Steve Cardamone, Bob Tucker and Kevin O'Donnell – made sure that Natalie would have the support she needed. They also made sure she didn't forget about her duties in the classroom.

For kids in crisis, it can be difficult to understand the relevance of learning algebraic equations or Constitutional amendments when something terrible and scary is haunting their lives. But the truth is that kids need to keep pace academically, even during the hard times, maybe even *especially* during the hard times. That's the message that a mentor can deliver.

There were times when I didn't want to push ahead, Natalie said of our Illinois team. *But they were constantly checking in and making sure I was okay and on track. They looked out for me.*

Natalie graduated from Illinois State University in 2014 with a degree in parks and recreation. She landed a job as the fitness director for the park district in Romeoville, Illinois.

She became a mentor herself for two high school girls. During tough times, when these girls wondered aloud about why so many things seemed to be going wrong, Natalie could summon her own experiences.

Life can be hard, she told them in a voice that was both gentle and strong. *But you just keep on going.*

Abby Turnbough was another student who knew grown-up troubles at a young age. Her dad was not a part of her life. Her mom, who never got the chance to go to college herself, worked two jobs to keep up with the bills. Hardest of all, Abby had watched two older siblings endure major health issues.

For Abby, it meant a lot to hear her mentor, Patricia Surman, simply tell her:

It's going to be okay.

If mentoring were an event in the Olympic Games, Surman, as an assistant principal at Lockport High School, would have been awarded the gold medal. We did the next best thing. Our foundation named her one of our two Mentors of the Year in 2016.

She was never afraid to pull a girl out of class to have a needed talk.

What's going on with your grades?

Are you feeling all right?

What's going on… really?

She would go to Rotary dinners to support her girls. She showed up at a big rally for the bowling team when they went to state. Abby was on the team, so she needed to be there for support. She acted as chaperone on student tours to colleges.

You don't have to be their best friend, Surman said. *You just want them to know you're there for them. You don't have all the answers – but you can get them an answer.*

When her siblings were going through medical issues, Abby missed some time from school. Surman was there to help Abby manage her school assignments – and act as a liaison with teachers – while the high school girl tended to her siblings.

Abby's grade point average rose to a lofty 3.8. She began to ponder a career in the medical field, largely because health care had mattered so much in the lives of her brother and sister.

The mentor program officially ends when the kids go off to college. But Taylore Gray, who enrolled at Loyola University in Chicago, knew she could still count on Patricia Surman.

She tells you how it is, said Taylore. *She tells you, 'You've got to get it together.'*

Not much has changed since high school days.

The only difference is that I used to call her Mrs. Surman, said Taylore, *and now I call her Trish.*

Michael Vitha-Nolan, a sophomore at Plainfield East High School, could feel the stress in the house. It was impossible to hide the worry when the family was in danger of losing their home. Both parents had been out of work for long periods with health problems, and possible foreclosure loomed.

A talented artist and swimmer, Michael had worried that there wouldn't be any money for college. After he interviewed with the Give Something Back Foundation, the shy young man came home with a smile and a scholarship.

I feel like a heavy weight has been lifted, he would say later.

As part of the deal, he was paired with a mentor, David Arnold.

The nice thing about having a mentor is that you've got somebody to be accountable to, said Michael's mom, Debbie. *It's one thing for a parent to say, 'You've got to get on that!' and it takes on another meaning when it's someone else saying it.*

When Michael was wavering about the importance of taking Spanish, it was Arnold who spoke up: *Colleges consider it very important to have taken a language in high school.* It was more than a suggestion. Michael respected Arnold's advice, so he signed up for Spanish.

Arnold would routinely drive to the Vitha-Nolan house for brunch, conversation and board games. He went to Michael's swim meets and art contests.

When Michael won induction into his school's Art National Honor Society – snagging a first place ribbon in his category – his parents were there with smiles. And so was his mentor, Arnold.

At just twenty-four, Sean Ruane was a mentor not far removed from his own high school days in Georgia. Like a lot of great mentors, he was able to draw on his own struggles and disappointments in empathizing with a mentee.

From the time he could walk, Ruane was playing ball with his dad, a man who had been a standout baseball player in high school and college, back in the day.

In Sean's early years, he was a star, too. In some eighth grade basketball games, he would pour in twenty points or more.

Sports were my world, he said. *It was my entire identity.*

That would make it all the tougher in his freshman year, he explained, when he was cut from the basketball team roster.

It was a devastating experience. That year, he had a class with a teacher who was also a coach. The teacher knew how much the young Ruane had been hurt.

He told him he understood the disappointment and that he shouldn't give up. Instead of feeling sorry for himself, the teacher told Ruane: *Work 100 times harder.*

He believed in me, said Ruane, *when I didn't believe in myself.*

Ruane went back at it the next season and made the basketball team. But he was cut once more as a junior. Worse yet, he was also cut from the baseball team.

Unwilling to give up, he played for club teams through high school. When he decided to enroll at Lewis University, he tried out for the baseball team as a walk-on, a player that has not been recruited by the college squad.

He made the team. He will never forget taking the field for Lewis, as his dad and the rest of the family cheered from the bleachers.

As he made his way through school, Ruane was drawn to mission work, especially for the cause of social justice. It ultimately eclipsed his desire to play baseball, so he left the team to have more time to serve others.

When he took a job at Lewis, Ruane saw an e-mail seeking mentors for the Give Something Back Foundation.

I jumped at it, he said.

He thought about his old teacher, the one who had helped him piece together his shattered self-image after being cut from the basketball team. A mentor, he knew, could change a life.

He was assigned to a teenager named Darnell Dail, who lived in a rough-at-the-edges neighborhood in Joliet, a town known mostly for its former state prison.

Darnell was an African American kid who stood 6'4" as a sophomore. When you're black and very tall, people ask you a lot about playing basketball.

It's usually the second question, said Darnell. *It gets irritating.*

Darnell had no interest in basketball – or stereotypes.

Quiet and artistic, he took a heavy load of honors and Advanced Placement classes: physics, geometry, French II, European history.

For a physics project, he devised a fifty-piece Rube Goldberg machine that he described as *the coolest thing I've done.*

When he was first assigned a mentor, he acknowledged being a bit skeptical.

How much time is this going to take? he wondered.

As it turned out, Darnell and the mentor, Ruane, really clicked.

In a way, they had a bit of a sports identity phenomenon in common. Ruane had once desperately wanted to be a star athlete more than anything in the world. The world, meanwhile, seemed to insist that Darnell be an athlete. But he recoiled at the *jockocracy*.

Both of them learned something about societal expectations – and themselves.

When they got together, Ruane talked a bit about his own experiences, but only when Darnell asked. He was careful about dispensing what he called *cheap advice*.

To hear Darnell tell it, the mentor was an all-star.

Hannah Thompson cannot walk or talk. She cannot feed herself or grasp a pen to write words on a page.

Despite all of that – and partially *because of* all of that – she was a brilliant communicator. She also became a mentor – and a motivational speaker – for the Give Something Back Foundation.

Hannah was a busy young woman. She worked as the social media director for the chamber of commerce in Chicago's hip River North neighborhood. She earned a bachelor's degree in communications from Elmhurst College, where she belonged to three honor societies.

She wrote a popular blog, *Hannah's Adventures of Living Her Dreams*. She traveled to Washington, DC, where she served on an advisory board for the Federal Communication Commission. Appointed to the panel at age twenty-four, she was the youngest member of the committee.

She was an emerging star in the motivational field, known for her presentation, "Do Your Impossible."

Hannah was born with cerebral palsy. Attached to her motorized wheelchair is a touch pad called a DynaVox.

She struggles mightily to coordinate her wavering arms. With her pink polished fingernails, she pecks at the keyboard on her machine and it speaks her words for her.

Some would say I'm crazy... maybe brave, she explained in a video titled, *An Extraordinary Life,* which was recorded at a reunion of her sorority sisters. *But the people who call me determined... they really know me.*

I am Hannah Thompson. I can't walk. I can't talk. But I live an extraordinary life, which I would not trade for anything. Walking and talking are not essential to a good life, as long as I am learning something new or speaking to people. Who would trade that?

Kevin O'Donnell, the director of mentoring at the foundation, met Hannah at Elmhurst College when she was a student at the school. At the time, O'Donnell was the Catholic chaplain at the school.

At a mass one Sunday evening, Hannah had rolled her wheelchair among the thirty or so students straggling through the church doors.

The chaplain asked the crowd for two volunteers willing to read from the pulpit.

No one wanted to read publicly.

And then Hannah struggled to raise her hand to volunteer. If no one else was willing to read, she could do it.

The chaplain, who knew Hannah as a friend, couldn't resist giving a gentle jibe to the other kids.

So the girl who can't talk – she's willing to read! he said. *I guess she called the rest of you out!*

Inspired by Hannah's courage, every student in the crowd quickly lifted a hand to read.

Hannah Marie Thompson was born June 25, 1990. It had been what medical professionals call a difficult birth. It became immediately apparent that the baby was having difficulty. Hannah could not take to the bottle. But doctors could not diagnose the eventual severity of her condition when her parents, Jean and Dan, took her home to the North Side of Chicago.

Over time, her physical limitations would become obvious – and so would her remarkable intellect.

Having cereal with her dad one morning, Hannah, not yet two years old, made an insistent motion to a letter in the newspaper, then jerked her gaze in her mom's direction, and motioned back to the letter in the newspaper.

It was the letter M, for mom. Before long, Hannah was communicating by spelling entire sentences, pointing to one letter at a time.

Letter by letter, her mom would recall, *she would spell, 'I want to go to the park.'*

As a little girl, Hannah had friends, but by middle school, most of them drifted away. A friend down the street stayed with her, but during the summer before freshman year, she came to the house and told Hannah that their kinship had run its course.

She dumped her, said Hannah's mom, Jean. *I wish there was a better way to put it. But that's what it was. She dumped her.*

In her high school years in north suburban Glenview, Hannah was isolated. Most of the disabled kids were cognitively delayed. Hannah saw herself as a normal kid. But the normal kids saw it otherwise.

Hannah tells people she understands the feeling of not fitting in.

I'm different, she said. *I have always been 'the different one...
the girl in the wheelchair... the kid who cannot walk or talk.'*

From an early age, Hannah had huge ambition.

*How can I be great at being the kid in the wheelchair? This is where
courage came in. It was essential that I had courage to be different.*

She decided to try out for the speech team.

That's right, she said with a smile, communicating through
her computerized device, *the speech team.*

She placed in three tournaments.

It gave me an identity other than just 'the girl in the wheelchair,'
she said. *Now, I was 'the girl in the wheelchair who was on the
speech team.'*

*Do you see what I did? I had an identity because of my physical
appearance, and then decided to link that to something else.*

She later volunteered for Onward House, a learning center
for underprivileged kids on the South Side of Chicago.
The volunteers would take a bus to the city and help young
students with homework.

*So now I was 'the kid in the wheelchair who was on the speech team
and volunteered at Onward House,'* she said. *See what I was doing?
I'm creating identities for myself besides 'the girl in the wheelchair.'*

During her high school commencement ceremony, the
principal announced to the audience with evident pride and
admiration that one of the graduates in the class had *overcome
insurmountable odds* and would now be going on to college.

Curious, Hannah looked around. She wondered who he
might have been talking about.

Her dad leaned over and explained that the principal was
talking about *Hannah.*

Here's the thing, Hannah explained. *My parents never said things like, 'You have insurmountable challenges' or 'You have such a hard life.'*

It was always, 'We will find a way' or 'You can do it.'

Hannah said she never looked at her disability as an obstacle or a challenge. Rather, it was *something to work with.*

The social aspect of high school had been difficult. Her fellow students were reluctant to hang with the girl in the wheelchair who couldn't talk.

I don't think they were mean-spirited, she said. *I think they were afraid.*

She wasn't bullied. Most of the time, she was just ignored.

At senior night, the party after high school graduation, there was no one to hang with Hannah. As she put it, the other kids couldn't grasp *how much fun being different could be.*

She ended up calling her parents and going home. She decided to simply move on.

When she enrolled at Elmhurst College, the world seemed to change. Other kids wanted to talk to her. They wanted to hang with her. It seemed as if *the storm stopped and I found the rainbow.*

Before long, however, the others moved to activities like dance or soccer, and Hannah was left alone.

Eager to expand her social life, she saw a poster for sorority recruitment and decided to rush two sororities.

She said she *poured my soul* into getting accepted to one of the sororities. Both rejected her.

I was heartbroken, she said.

She began to second-guess everything about herself and her choices in life. Her confidence took a hit. She seriously wondered if going to Elmhurst College had been a mistake. Her mom urged her to push ahead.

A few months later, a new sorority came to campus, looking for recruits. Hannah decided to give it a try. Her parents were reluctant, telling her that the sorority world was probably not ready for a girl like her. Hannah knew she might face another rejection. But she was not going to live her life in fear and regret.

I knew I had to try, she said.

So she took a chance.

Hannah won acceptance to the Phi Mu sorority, and by the end of her first year, she won the coveted Sisterhood Award.

She also served in the student government, belonged to three honor societies and participated in the Catholic Student Association.

I am humbled by Hannah's service for Give Something Back and by the way she describes the work of the foundation. *It is a mission,* she said, *founded on the value of grace.*

Hannah began serving as a mentor to Abbigail Suda, a student at Romeoville High School and a Give Something Back scholar.

Every time I talk to Hannah, said Abbigail, *I learn something about life.*

Abbigail was a National Honor Society student and a soccer player. She hoped someday to become a nurse practitioner or perhaps a radiologist.

She and Hannah would get together at Starbucks, but they also regularly communicated through texts.

Abbigail knew that Hannah was always there when she needed her.

When things get stressful, she just tells me to just take a step back and take a breath, said Abbigail, who lived in a modest home with her mom, her brother and her brother's friend. *Honestly, Hannah has accomplished so much in her life. She inspires me. I think that if she could go to college, so can I.*

Like our other mentors, Hannah was leading our students to places they might never have imagined they could reach.

I don't want to blend in, explained the self-described 'girl in the wheelchair.'

I want to stand out.

CHAPTER ELEVEN

THE SOCIAL COSTS FOR FIRST-GENERATION COLLEGE KIDS

Stephanie FigPope grew up in a duplex in Miami, sharing a bedroom with her mother and a younger brother. When she arrived on the campus of Columbia College in New York, she found herself surrounded by wealthy students who were *speaking a language I didn't know.*

I would mispronounce words that I'd read, but never heard spoken out loud when I was growing up, because there was no one around to correct me, said Stephanie. *People would talk about books they all knew. I remember thinking, 'What is this book, "The Little Prince," that everybody seems to have read as a kid?'*

Stephanie was smart enough to compete in the classroom. But there was no way she could keep up with the free-spending lifestyle of wealthy classmates.

I lost a lot of friends my freshman year, she said. *They weren't being mean or anything. It's just that they would do things I couldn't afford – going out for dinner, movies. After a while, they stopped asking me. Even if they were just hanging out in their dorm rooms at night, they didn't invite me anymore.*

Students on tight budgets at expensive colleges refer to it as *social weeding*, a process of culling by economic class, even if it's done unintentionally. If you can't spend, you can't hang.

When peers at Columbia invited Stephanie to join them for dinner, she made excuses about homework.

Didn't you just eat out last night? Stephanie remembered thinking to herself silently. But she would never have spoken such words. *It would have been too embarrassing to say, 'I just can't afford to go.' Rich students just wouldn't understand that. They'd think, 'Come on, it's not a big deal – it's just going out to eat!'*

On a rare occasion, Stephanie would join friends in going to an inexpensive Indian restaurant and search for the cheapest appetizer on the menu, spreading it out on her plate to make it look like a main course.

For students of modest means, even if they are attending school on a full scholarship, there is little room in the budget for frills that affluent kids take for granted at college.

I couldn't do 99 percent of the things my classmates were doing, said Stephanie.

Wealthy students, meaning no harm, make casual references to their upbringing as children of privilege. They might toss off comments about the works of Monet or Descartes. Maybe they will make small talk about a trip to Naples or Buenos Aires. Perhaps they will share memories of seeing a performance by Itzhak Perlman.

In these conversations, the children of plumbers and secretaries and housekeepers tend to keep silent, at a loss to join in the conversation, and worried that they are about to be discovered as pretenders in the ranks of these poised young Ivy Leaguers.

As a way to share, and sometimes vent, without risking public humiliation, some poor and working-class students started a Facebook page about the challenges and culture shock of being surrounded by affluence. It was called Columbia University Class Confessions.

I'm trying so hard not to be ashamed of being poor, one student posted, *since shame is such a dirty, unnecessary feeling, but it's really freaking hard…. I just recently found out that a bunch of my friends get FB notifications when I post in the meal exchange program and it made me want to cry.*

Others wrote about the condescension they would hear from rich students speaking in stereotypes when talking about the working class. It stings, they said, and taking part in such talk makes them feel disloyal to family and friends back home.

It really bothers me when my friends here bash people who go to community colleges or state schools, one student posted on Confessions. *Most of my friends from my public high school went to either a community college or state school, and they are all smart, talented people who could do well anywhere they went. I'm always uncomfortable talking about my friends back home because I don't want them to be unfairly judged.*

Some of the posts revealed a constant, urgent sense of worry about money, even doom.

Financial aid letters are going to be coming soon and my mom and I are terrified, one student shared in a post. *What if it's way more than we can pay? I don't even want to think about what I have to do if that happened.*

The postings also told secrets of students who were hustling as hard as they could to make money and good grades, sometimes to the point of exhaustion and desperation.

Today I slept through my alarm clock and missed a quiz, another post on Confessions shared. *I've been working three jobs in addition to classes and I crashed. I don't know what to do.*

Some poorer kids acknowledged being irked by affluent students who voice a commitment to equality and global social justice and then, in another breath, make snide remarks about people who live in trailer parks.

Everyone is acting progressive about 'the struggle,' one working-class student observed on the page, *but they aren't fixing the little things that make poor students feel excluded and hurt.*

One student posted that he tried to hide the details of his humble background from friends, worried that it would color their perceptions about him and his intellect.

People look at you differently when they know you're poor, he wrote. *You suddenly go from 'Damn, Tom is smart and cool' to 'Damn, Tom is smart for a poor kid.'*

In the worst of cases, poorer students interpret setbacks as proof that they don't really belong in the smart, high-stepping world of the academic elite.

Coming here has made me into a failure... pretty sure I just bombed one of my exams... low-income and unable to compete with my classmates.

The Columbia University Class Confessions page, along with whispered talk about the fears of students without money, helped spark the formation of a new support group on campus, First-Generation Low-Income Partnership.

Lizette Delgadillo was the president of the group, known as FLIP. She grew up in East Los Angeles, the daughter of a housekeeper.

It started with five people sitting in a student lounge, said Lizette, an engineering and biomedical sciences major at Columbia. *We were talking about what it's like to be a first-generation college or low-income student. Someone pointed out that there are groups for every racial, ethnic and religious group, but not one for people like us.*

These were students, she said, who deserved a voice and a community to fight the sense of isolation. Similar groups have organized at other prestigious colleges, including Harvard and Brown, which draw heavily from wealthy boarding schools and upscale suburbs.

The issue went viral after a Duke University student, KellyNoel Waldorf, wrote a guest column about her experiences of being poor among wealthy classmates:

In my four years at Duke, I have tried to write this article many times. But I was afraid. I was afraid to reveal an integral part of myself. I'm poor.

Being a student from economic struggle, it became clear to her, was not something to advertise.

While writing my resume, I put McDonald's under work experience. A friend leaned over and said, 'Do you think it's a good idea to put that on your resume?' In their eyes, it was better to list no work experience than to list this 'lowly' position.

In the newspaper column, she wrote that she hoped to reach out to other students from poorer backgrounds who were frustrated in trying to find a way among the socially elite.

If you have ever felt like this important piece of your identity was not welcome at Duke, know that you are not the only one. I want you to know that 'poor' is not a dirty word.... I want to say to you that no matter what socioeconomic status you come from, your experiences are worthy. And because no one in four years has said it yet to me: It's okay to be poor and go to Duke.

At Columbia University, a majestically Gothic campus on the Upper West Side of Manhattan, some students strolling between classes could be mistaken for fashion models, adorned in designer outfits and boots that cost thousands of dollars.

Some students of modest means, on the other hand, struggle to come up with a hundred bucks needed for an inexpensive, but sturdy winter coat for that howling nor'easter.

For those on a tight budget, the First-Generation organization on campus committed to distributing heavy coats donated by other students. The group also coordinated a textbook rental program, helping students who could scarcely afford $300 for a new chemistry book.

The fledgling group found an ally in Cristen Kromm, the dean of undergraduate student life, who has walked in their shoes. A first-generation college student, she was raised by a single mother.

As an economically struggling undergraduate at Wheaton College in Massachusetts, she remembered friends who had houses on Cape Cod and traveled around the world.

And I was babysitting to earn some money, she recalled.

Dean Kromm believes that schools like Columbia, which granted official status to the First-Generation Low-Income Partnership organization, has made strides to become more aware about economic diversity, *but there's a way to go.*

In an article headlined, "What Is It Like to Be Poor at an Ivy League School?" Ana Barros told a *Boston Globe* reporter she saw *class markers everywhere,* from speech to dinner table manners.

When Julia Dixon enrolled at Yale University, her parents rented a car and drove up from Georgia. The parents felt a bit intimidated by their daughter's upscale classmates and professors. They sought out the kitchen help.

Her dad asked the short-order cooks, *Can you look out for my baby?*

For some students who made it from modest backgrounds to fancy colleges, it can feel like they fit in neither place.

Poorer students go to school with wealthy classmates who cannot fathom their working-class lives. And then they return home to places that don't want a highfalutin college boy or girl putting on any airs.

As KellyNoel put it:

I am scared that the more I increase my 'social mobility,' the further I will separate myself from my family.

One blue-collar dad told his daughter, *I don't want you to be ashamed of us.*

As a low-income student, Stephanie FigPope landed a Work Study job swiping security cards at university buildings. She appreciated the work because she needed the money, but she always worried that she might need to swipe the card of someone she knew. And when she did recognize a face, it was an awkward exchange.

A peer would occasionally comment, with a tone of surprise, *Oh, you're Work Study.* She knew that was code for being poor.

As a kid who worked in food service at the University of Illinois, so many years before, I knew very well what social class was doing the kitchen work on campus. Two months into my freshman year at the University of Illinois, I was back in the kitchen of my dorm complex with the other ninety cent per hour workers when we learned that John Kennedy had been assassinated. My more affluent peers were having lunch with one another in the front of the cafeteria. That illustrated the class divide. Despite being college boys, we thought of ourselves as working-class kids.

While other students flew home for breaks or long weekends, Stephanie stayed in the dorms, quiet except for the occasional international student. On Christmas Day, she was relieved to be assigned to work, earning time-and-a-half pay on a holiday. In this small way, she was following in the footsteps of her mom, a nursing assistant in the cancer ward of Mercy Hospital, who regularly worked on holidays.

On Parents' Weekend, there was no way Stephanie's mother or father could afford to come to visit.

Stephanie's parents, who divorced when she was seven years old, scrimped to attend her commencement. After her college graduation, she and her dad dined at a restaurant, where some friends in New York kindly picked up the tab. A few days later, after the university-wide commencement, she and her mother walked several blocks away from campus, in search of a cheap sushi restaurant to celebrate her academic triumph.

Stephanie, who is now a successful photographer, has every right to be proud. But her accomplishments leave her torn.

I feel guilty, so terribly guilty, she said, her voice trembling. *There are so many people just like me who could have gotten into Columbia, but they just didn't get lucky.*

She says she has often sought refuge in talking with others at prestigious schools that also came from modest backgrounds and have struggled with feelings of being unworthy.

My friends and I talk about this all the time, said Stephanie. *Why did we get to go to an Ivy League school while the others – our cousins, our friends – are working at minimum wage jobs? We try to reassure each other that we really do deserve it. But it's hard. You go from being poor to having more money than your parents have.*

While Stephanie didn't have the money to join her friends on evenings out, she met another student with empty pockets, a young man named Andrew.

The two of them would spend hours talking about their backgrounds, and found they had a lot in common. Andrew's family had gone through a home foreclosure. They bonded in conversations about the best places and events to find free food.

When others went out on the town, Andrew and Stephanie would go for walks and talks. And their dates tended to center around studying.

The way she saw the world, and what was important, Andrew said of Stephanie, *I thought she was pretty cool.*

On New Year's Eve of 2014, they were married at City Hall. They combined their names – Fig from Stephanie's last name and Pope from Andrew's – to create a new surname.

To celebrate their nuptials, they joined five or six other friends at a tapas restaurant, and *then went back to the apartment and just chilled.*

The following July, they took a honeymoon trip to Colorado and Utah on the cheap, visiting national parks and camping or sleeping in the car to save on lodging costs.

When Andrew took a job as a software engineer, and Stephanie worked as a photographer, the two of them were able to live in an apartment on the East Side of Manhattan.

It was a sweet start for a young couple who knew the value of hard work and sacrifice.

They should stop feeling guilty.

CHAPTER TWELVE

DRAWING STRENGTH FROM HARDSHIP

Shame is corrosive and debilitating. And so often it is completely irrational. For kids who have known economic hardship, or their parents, there is no reason to feel embarrassed about their financial circumstances. And yet, so many do.

When I was very young, I had worshiped my father – or at least worshiped the idea of a dad I could idolize. I remember my friends giving me a hard time for putting him on such a pedestal.

Why do you talk so much about your dad? an exasperated friend once challenged me.

And it was true. I made him into a hero because I wanted him to be a hero. And I desperately wanted him to be proud of me.

As I look back on the life of my dad, I now see a scared man who carried a lot of shame. Life had seemed to mock him, and he answered with bluster and bitterness. And people who did not go to college tend to know that plenty of educated people look down on them.

My father had grown up with some big dreams. A handsome, swaggering young man who cruised on a roaring motorcycle, he had readied himself for a high-stepping future. He was certain that one day he would be calling the shots and counting his money.

He had scarcely intended to become a lackey, as he described it, a blue-collar stiff at the Argonne National Laboratory. As he saw it, some highfalutin professionals at the lab, perhaps some with doctoral degrees, treated him as a nobody. It was honorable work, and required no apologies.

My dad also worked moonlight jobs. He served drinks at Lennie's Bar and pumped gas at the Standard Oil station. It was a testament to his work ethic, but I'm sure he saw those jobs as evidence of his failure.

He bragged that he had never read a book in his life. He had a stable government job until he retired at age sixty-two. He was never proud of the job or himself.

He was a miserable man. It didn't have to be that way. But it was that way. He would escape, temporarily, by crawling into bottles of Jim Beam, and then permanently, by taking his life.

Unfortunately, many have accepted the bogus, but widespread notion that people whose bank accounts are worth less (or worth nothing) are themselves worth less (or worth nothing). It is a profanity to make sport of people because they live in poverty, and yet terms like *ghetto* become adjectives and *trailer trash* reduces human beings to rubbish.

Treated as an outcast, a person is far more likely to turn to antisocial behavior, especially if they feel blocked from constructive paths like good jobs and college education.

Is it any wonder that so many people in despair numb themselves with drugs? Or turn to a life of crime? Or simply give in and go through the motions, enduring jobs they hate, day after day, as my own parents did?

For young people in trying circumstances, the truth is that David can outduel Goliath. Young people from modest means should see their working-class wisdom as an asset.

A bright young person in hardship can catch up with the cultural and social knowledge taken for granted by those who started life in a place of comfort. But it doesn't work the other way around. Some things cannot be divined from books. A wealthy person will never really be able to genuinely learn what it's like to struggle economically.

Growing up hardscrabble, learning to make your way without much in the way of material comforts, can teach you powerful insights about life. You gain some vital survival skills that can be enriching at school and the workplace. It can help you see beyond designer brands and fancy pedigrees.

When my company was hit by an international hacking scheme, and I lost all of my hundreds of millions of dollars of paper wealth, some well-meaning people tried to console me.

They all took for granted that this was surely the worst experience I had ever known. But it wasn't. I remember thinking to myself: *If you had grown up in the home where I did, you'd know better than to ask that question.*

How bad is this? Would I rather be here or back as an eight-year-old in my childhood home, with no confidence, and nowhere to turn?

I'd choose to stay put.

The world is full of young, unsung working-class heroes. The teenager who has stayed home during the evenings, in order to serve as the supervising adult for younger siblings, while a single parent is at work on the graveyard shift; the kid who resisted the entreaties of street gangs, and instead took a job flipping burgers; the person who changed schools mid-semester, time and again, while being passed from Mom's apartment to Dad's place, and then to Grandma's home, all the while keeping up with her homework.

CHAPTER THIRTEEN

DINNER PARTY PREP SCHOOL

Under the soft light of chandeliers, the working-class teenagers sat stiffly at their formal dinner settings, more than a little self-conscious in the white linen environs. It was an event sponsored by our foundation that we dubbed Etiquette Night.

As scholarship winners in the Give Something Back scholarship program, these were bright and hardworking students from families who live paycheck-to-paycheck and did not spend a lot of time in fancy restaurants. They were getting a rare chance to learn about dinner party manners in a formal setting.

Children of privilege learn early the customs of gentility, from knowing how to don appropriate formal wear to being fluent in table manners. These are the niceties that help people climb the social and economic ladder in America.

Blue-collar kids tend to grow up relatively clueless about such social cues. One working-class young man, raised in the rural Midwest, confessed to being rattled during a job interview at a fancy French restaurant with a coterie of company managers. When he opened the menu, none of the offerings were familiar to his meat-and-potatoes upbringing. More alarming still, he didn't know the proper way of eating whatever it was that he would be served (he knew enough to know that parts of certain delicacies were not to be eaten at all).

Relying on his wiles, he ordered the identical selection as one chosen by one of the bosses, and then he imitated every move of the fork and knife made by the proper gentleman.

The prosperous and socially well-bred often fail to recognize that such manners have been taught to them as part of the happy accident of being born into a certain social class.

For Etiquette Night, we hired a team of experts on manners to meet with the scholarship students at DiNolfo's, a nice banquet hall in a leafy suburb south of Chicago. The kids learned about how to handle everything from the soup spoon and salad fork, to engaging in small talk with strangers.

The focus on dinner table manners and social etiquette might seem odd for a foundation devoted to scholarships for the underprivileged. But most working-class kids, including me, know the anxiety – and often incompetence – of trying to mingle in more polished society.

Whether or not such social dexterity *should* matter, it *does* matter. Self-confidence is among the most important attributes. People judge others based on their confidence, as well as the way he or she speaks, dresses and eats. In a lunch or dinner with a college admissions official or alumni, manners count for a lot – just as they do in business or, for that matter, on a date (poor manners can make a first date the last one).

On Etiquette Night, our students arrived looking sharp. We didn't require suits or elegant dresses. Many of our students don't have such articles in their closets. But they showed up well-groomed and respectably dressed.

To set them at ease, the students were greeted by an etiquette expert who reminded them:

Don't worry about making mistakes. No one expects you to know this. You will be learning by doing. It's like a foreign language. If you practice, it will become part of your life.

And then she made a key point, something the kids knew instinctively, but were glad to hear:

All the etiquette in the world doesn't matter if you're not kind and respectful. That's what people remember.

They were reminded to introduce themselves when they arrived at a table, and to remember the five Ss when they make an acquaintance: stand, smile, see, shake and say something.

The expert told the students to look directly at the person being greeted, paying close enough attention to know the color of his or her eyes.

And so the kids mingled around the table, following the prompts.

Nice to meet you, one of the boys said to a girl nearby, with a smile and an outstretched hand.

The drill was repeated throughout the room, and almost everyone followed the strict advice against looking down at your shoes.

There were other important rules to be observed, including some that go against the grain of society these days: *Don't read or send a text… or take a call.*

Nothing was to be placed on the table – no phones, no purses, no notebooks. Napkins were to be placed on laps, with the four corners pointed inward, so they could dab their mouths more easily.

And then came the discussion about the utensils – which ones to use, and how to use them, and for which dishes. It could all get tricky, the etiquette expert conceded, and reminded them that they were not alone in feeling anxious. It was not the end of the world if they made a mistake.

The students learned about the American zigzag style of eating and the Continental custom. They were reminded to rest the knife on the plate with the jagged side pointed inward.

How many of you eat like this at home? the expert asked.

Not a hand went up.

The ability to make conversation, they were told, was crucial. The best way to be a good conversationalist was to be a good listener, to ask questions, and to make sure that everyone at the table was getting a chance to participate in the conversation.

Sitting among them was an honor student named Emmanuel Mendez. He was attending as a student at Joliet West High School. He lived with a brother and two cousins, along with his mother, Josephine, and his stepfather, Tedoro.

Emmanuel was only three years old when he lost his father, Guillermo. His dad was a member of the Latin Kings street gang. He was shot to death in an altercation with the police.

The son has only flashes of memories of his father. Most are vague. But one recollection is vivid.

I remember staring at the open casket, he said.

After the Etiquette Dinner, Emmanuel routinely practiced the manners he learned during every dinner at home.

His mom, Josephine, who never finished high school, practiced table manners alongside him. She has never had much money, but she has invested a lot in her son. She moved the family from an apartment in a dangerous, gang-ridden neighborhood to a safer section of town in Joliet. She was determined that *history will not repeat itself.*

Despite knowing tragedy so early in his life, Emmanuel was a kid who talked more about opportunities than disadvantages. He was determined to go to college and eventually become a physician.

Everybody experiences adversity, he said. *It comes in different ways. But adversity is part of everybody's life.*

CHAPTER FOURTEEN

SWEAT AND SMARTS

Most students have never heard of a Work College, and most young people raised in affluence would not likely consider attending such a school.

Elizabeth Quick was not wealthy, nor was she afraid of hard work. It was big student debt that scared her.

With keys hanging from her belt, and her clothes splattered with paint, Elizabeth climbed down from a ladder in a student dormitory and wiped the sweat off her brow. She was working on drywall, or sheetrock, as it's called in the building trades.

For affordable tuition, Elizabeth was working part-time on a construction site at Blackburn College in rural Illinois. The liberal arts college is one of seven federally subsidized Work Colleges in the United States.

At Blackburn, like other work schools, everyone has a job. It's the way that these academically strong colleges are able to hold down tuition costs for their bright, unspoiled students.

These are colleges for smart kids who are unaccustomed to privilege. As the college adage has it: *Blackburn is a school for students who have everything but money.*

The school sits on an eighty-acre campus of trees and rolling hills in Illinois coal country near the small town of Carlinville. It has an enrollment of about 550.

Elizabeth, a computer science major with plans to become a web designer or programmer, came from a high school class of thirty-seven students in Ashland, Illinois. Her parents didn't make a lot of money and there wasn't any extra for college. She chose Blackburn, intent on becoming the first member of her family to earn a bachelor's degree.

She remembered some peers in high school giving her a curious look when she talked about her plans to attend a college that would require her to work ten hours a week as part of her tuition payment.

But less than four years later, as she neared college graduation, Elizabeth was grateful that she had only a couple of thousand dollars in student loans. Some of her friends from back home, meanwhile, were saddled with student debt that approached or exceeded $100,000.

People are jealous of me, said Elizabeth, twenty, trying to suppress a smile, as she climbed the ladder and went back to work.

This liberal arts college is an example of how students of modest means can attend college without taking on massive debt. Graduates of Blackburn, who predominantly grow up in working-class families, leave school with student debt that is less than half the national average owed by graduates.

The other work colleges in the United States include Alice Lloyd College and Berea College, both in Kentucky, College of the Ozarks in Missouri, Ecclesia College in Arkansas,

Sterling College in Vermont, and Warren Wilson College in North Carolina.

Blackburn, a school that is highly respected for its mission and its academic rigor, is one of the partner colleges with the Give Something Back Foundation.

This school has plenty of success stories. Its alumni include Senator Mark Kirk of Illinois, Craig Stowers, the chief justice of the Supreme Court in Alaska, and Walt Harrington, the Emmy-winning documentarian, journalist and professor.

Another proud alum is Bob Tucker, a farm boy who would rise to become a college admissions officer, before ultimately taking the reins as the deputy director at the Give Something Back Foundation. He graduated from Blackburn in 1984.

Blackburn is more affordable than most residential colleges. For the 2016–17 school year, tuition, room and board is about $28,000. Students willing to live in a dorm without air conditioning get a discount of $700. The school fosters an egalitarian culture. When every student sees every other student pulling weeds, painting a wall, digging a ditch or washing dishes, it becomes evident that *no human being,* as my mother used to say, *is more important or less important than another human being.*

It is a culture that stands in contrast to the social and economic distinctions that prevail at many schools. Laura Hamilton, a sociologist and associate professor at the University of California, Merced, described the stark economic class divisions at many colleges in an article published in 2015 in the *Wall Street Journal.*

Residential colleges often resemble luxury cruise liners, Professor Hamilton wrote. *A subset of affluent students are there to have the time of their lives. They eat, study and play in a world*

*serviced by others. Less-advantaged students and staff serve them
their meals, pick up their towels at the gym, reshelve their books in
the library and fill their beers in the local bar.*

At Blackburn, those economic class lines are blurred to
the point of being invisible. No student can skip the work
requirement by paying a higher tuition. It is not an option.
Besides the required ten hours of work each week that goes
toward tuition costs, students have the option to work up to
ten more hours a week to earn some spending money.

A central tenet at Blackburn is that *all* work deserves
honor and dignity, and that no job should be regarded with
the pejorative of being menial, according to the school's
president, John Comerford.

He tells students:

*As a college graduate, you will likely never work a job cleaning
toilets. But someone will. And it is important that you value that work.*

At Blackburn, coming from the working class is a source of
pride. That's not to suggest that affluence is viewed negatively.
Indeed, many Blackburn students say they fully hope to become
financially successful themselves someday. But no student at this
school is measured by the worth of a bank account, much less a
parents' bank account.

*We don't care what kind of car you drive, or the size of the house
that you came from,* said Dr. Comerford. *That lack of snobbery is
one of our greatest assets.*

Students at Blackburn display an unusual sense of ownership
of their college and campus. That is because, in large part, they
built it.

At the entrance of Ludlum Hall, a handsome brick building with arching windows, a bronze plaque notes the evident pride: *This building was constructed 1961–1966 by Blackburn students.*

On the current campus, nine of the major buildings have been built by students, under the direction of professional construction workers. Students maintain the grounds, cook the food and staff the administrative offices.

The school was established in 1837 and named for Gideon Blackburn, a Presbyterian minister known for gifted oratory, crafty real estate deals, and according to lore, a lucrative sideline business in running bourbon in counties where liquor was illegal.

In the early years, the school focused on training young men for the ministry, as did many colleges. By 1912, when Dr. William Hudson arrived at Blackburn as president, the college had fallen on hard times. Its assets had dwindled to less than $100,000. In 1913, Hudson created a work program for those who demonstrated academic prowess, but who lacked financial resources. It would become the hallmark of the college.

Newspaper accounts of college kids rolling up their sleeves and doing manual labor, it turned out, sparked widespread admiration, as Blackburn won donations from many businesses and individual philanthropists. The Pullman Company donated two of its passenger cars to the college in 1914, and the undergraduates fashioned them into student housing.

The sense of work and community permeates everyday life at Blackburn. When a violent storm roared through campus, knocking down many tree limbs and making a mess of the grounds, students poured out of the dormitories and began the cleanup effort.

There had been no orders or call for help. The students jumped to action, some of them later explained with a shrug, simply because the place belongs to them and they feel a responsibility to care for it.

Each of the seven federally subsidized Work Colleges around the nation has its own distinctive culture, as one college administrator put it, ranging from *right-wing conservative* to *left-wing granola*.

Blackburn draws students from Illinois farm country, big suburban high schools and hardscrabble Chicago neighborhoods. The college is racially diverse, and prides itself on embracing differences of all kinds.

A bulletin board on campus displayed a drawing of Rosie the Riveter, the classic muscle-flexing symbol of can-do spirit. It was posted by an organization called Society of Empowered Women, and a short text beneath the image explained its role:

We are supportive and nonjudgmental, with open minds and honest conversations.

President Comerford noted: *You might not expect to have a vibrant LGBT community here in rural Carlinville, Illinois, but we're happy that we do.*

As students attending a Work College (*Earn to Learn*, as a Blackburn tee shirt proclaims), these are individuals who have chosen a path regarded as unconventional, and so any other differences among them really don't seem to matter much.

Plenty of students at other colleges work at jobs, too, of course. But it is Blackburn's contention that students who work under college supervision fare better than those who work off campus. Supervisors on campus – often students themselves –

keep in mind that classroom work is the top priority. That might not be the case at the pizzeria in town that needs a waitress to pull a double shift, no matter that final exams are looming.

When students are working under the direction of people affiliated with the college, Comerford noted, an early warning system exists to detect when someone is facing extracurricular pressures. If a student is feeling distressed because a sibling is having legal trouble, for example, or parents are divorcing – or if students themselves are engaging in self-destructive behavior – the college can more quickly catch wind of the problem and provide the necessary guidance and support.

In part because so many of its students are the first in the family to attend college, Blackburn implements an intensive monitoring and mentoring program for freshmen. Comerford said the encouragement aims to ward off the *impostor syndrome*, the deep down fear among many working-class kids that they really aren't smart enough to be in college.

As soon as an accepted student puts down a deposit for enrollment, an academic advisor will be calling with congratulations and helpful insights and suggestions. And the calls keep coming.

New students are counseled during summer orientation and during move-in week. Through the first semester, students meet with advisors every couple of weeks to mull their experiences thus far and discuss their plans for the future.

We've found that if you can get a freshman to March in decent shape, said Comerford, *they're going to be fine.*

To judge from a student like Clark Johnson, who was majoring in political science, Blackburn students leave campus ready and eager to take on the world.

Clark, the son of a machinist and a school secretary, planned to go to law school, and someday make a name in politics.

I tell everyone I want to be president, said Clark, a campus grounds crew worker in a John Deere cap, jeans and work boots. *But I'll settle for the US Senate.*

Washington, DC would have to wait. Break time was over. Clark nodded in the direction of a yellow lawn tractor.

My horse awaits me, he explained.

CHAPTER FIFTEEN

FINDING THE PATH THROUGH COMMUNITY COLLEGE

As incoming high school freshmen and their parents listened, an educator was giving advice about the appropriate classes to take *if you want to go to 'real college' – you know, not 'community college.'*

Kristin O'Keefe, who was in the audience, bristled at the condescending remarks.

While O'Keefe did not go to a community college, as she wrote later in an essay for the *Motherlode* blog in the *New York Times* in 2015, she worked at one.

So did I.

Parkland College in Illinois was new in the late '60s when I took a job there. At the wise old age of twenty-one, I had been hired as a mathematics instructor. Within months, I was promoted to director of the computer center.

Like O'Keefe, I can attest that community colleges are full of bright, hardworking, purposeful students and teachers. Community college *is* real college.

Indeed, nearly half of all undergraduates in America today attend a community college, some seven million students. Community colleges, with a policy of admitting all students at a cost of about $4,000 a year for a full-time student, represent a path to higher education for those who do not have the money – or perhaps the high school grades, test scores or preparedness – to attend a four-year university. Still others could qualify and afford starting at a more expensive four-year university right after high school, but have decided to pursue a more frugal academic route.

For many other students, the value of a community college lies in the associate's degree, which is usually achievable in two years, if approached at a full-time clip.

The associate's degree opens doors to attractive jobs in many sectors, including health care, manufacturing, agribusiness and transportation. It also means a savings in opportunity costs. By entering the job market after two years, the associate graduates are already busy earning salaries while their peers at four-year institutions are still paying for classes in junior and senior year, often through expensive loans.

A community college like Parkland, located in Champaign, inevitably contends with living in the shadow of the University of Illinois at Urbana-Champaign. But plenty of Parkland's graduates have landed jobs and wages that might elicit envy among some of the alums who earned degrees across town at the more prominent Big Ten school.

Kassie Sturdyvin graduated from Parkland College in 2015 with an associate's degree in dental hygiene. She had worked hard in courses that included pharmacology, local anesthetics, English, speech and oral and dental anatomy.

The anatomy courses, she said, with a groan, *were really tough.* It paid off.

On the day of commencement, she received an e-mailed invitation to interview for a hygienist position with a dentist near

Champaign. A week later, she was offered a slot in an occupation with salaries that typically range from $45,000 to $60,000 a year, and sometimes more.

And get this: She works Monday through Thursday. She has Fridays off.

Kassie and her fiancé, Kody, are living proof that a community college degree can lead to a financially rewarding life.

Kody, a graduate of Danville Area Community College in Illinois, earns $65,000 as a wind turbine technician. Between the two of them, Kassie, twenty-two, and Kody, twenty-five, earn a six-figure household income.

They recently bought a comfortable, newer home with more than five acres of countryside property. Kody is an avid golfer, so they installed a putting green in the back yard.

The young couple has been able to save a substantial sum, but they can afford to splurge, too. They have taken two trips on cruise ships in the Caribbean, and were already planning a third vacation at sea. They also have taken occasional weekend trips to places like Las Vegas and Orlando.

It helps that Kody and Kassie, who lived at home during community college, graduated with no student debt – absolutely zero.

That was not the experience of Kassie's older sister, Kammie, twenty-five, who went to that prominent flagship school in Champaign.

Kammie graduated from the University of Illinois in 2013 with a bachelor's degree in psychology. She owed tens of thousands of dollars in student loans. For two years, she had been unable to find a job that required a college degree. She worked as a waitress at two restaurants in Iowa.

She is really smart, said Kassie, *but she's so frustrated.*

Seamus Reilly, a vice president at Parkland, is an Irish immigrant who obtained his undergraduate diploma in Dublin and his master's degree and PhD at Illinois. He encouraged his son to start at a community college.

We have a huge disconnect in society between education and work and skills, he said. *A bachelor's degree doesn't lead to a job. It's the skills that lead to a job. But in our society, we've been sold on the idea of 'the college experience' as going away to a four-year school. It's good marketing. It makes a lot of people a lot of money. But as far as the educational value, I'm not so sure.*

Reilly is busy fielding calls from employers in desperate need of workers.

Companies are worried about the aging work force, he said. *They're looking to us for students with strong math and critical thinking skills.*

These associate degree students are needed in fields like precision agriculture at big corporate farms. In manufacturing, moreover, it's not uncommon to have openings that pay $60,000 a year, with another $20,000 in overtime.

This isn't just kid stuff. Many of the Parkland students are in their late twenties, thirties, even forties. They have returned to school to augment skills that will make them more competitive and perhaps gain promotions and fatter paychecks.

I know of a single mother with a low-paying job who was having a very difficult time making ends meet, said Reilly, who watched as the woman earned an associate's degree that lifted her to the middle class. *It's changed the trajectory of her whole family. I remember her telling me proudly, 'Now, my children will be able to go to college.'*

For those with discipline and drive, community college can be a smart, affordable vehicle for getting ahead in life. But without specific goals and perseverance, it can also be a place where too many get stuck, or go dangerously in reverse.

According to figures from the Education Department, only 21 percent of full-time students at community colleges achieve a degree within three years. For students who took out loans, quitting school often spells disaster. According to a study by the Association of Community College Trustees, almost 90 percent of borrowers who default on loans were former students who left college with no degree or certificate of any kind. And borrowers from community colleges are the most likely to default on loans.

Like their working-class peers at four-year schools, community college students tend to have relatively little financial cushion. Any significant financial setback can lead to dropping out. Community college students often leave school simply because they are needed to work to support themselves and their families.

It is a common misconception that the most personally ruinous debts are those in the range of $100,000 or even $200,000, borrowed to attend elite universities, according to a study by Stanford University and the US Department of the Treasury. To the contrary, these researchers found default rates were lowest at selective four-year schools (6 percent) and highest at community colleges (31 percent). The study also found that borrowers with a comparatively low debt, about $8,000, were the most common to default.

It is a painful cycle. Community college students often struggle financially from the start. If they accrue debt and then leave school before graduating, they enter the job market without the qualifications to land a higher-paying job. Working at a low-wage job, in turn, makes it more difficult to pay down student debt. And when a former student goes into default on the loans, the penalties and interest rapidly become overwhelming.

The spiral underscores the role of class in the likelihood of earning a degree. Students from families with means are less likely to borrow and less likely to drop out. And they would be much more likely to be able to count on a parent or relative if they did fall behind on a debt.

An affluent family would be far less apt to let a $5,000 student debt become the cause of the ruin of financial and credit history. These families would be much more likely to have the means to pay off the debt, or at least bring the payments current.

Unless money is no object, community college is not usually a good place to simply chill out, and wait for inspiration to strike. But the same could be said of a four-year university.

Like all avenues of higher education, community college can be a gateway to career fulfillment and financial security, as long as it is pursued with good planning and a high level of motivation.

When Caitlyn Cordell graduated from Sherrard High School in rural Illinois, she wanted to enroll at the University of Iowa. Her parents cautioned her that out-of-state tuition would amount to a fortune. But Caitlyn's heart was set. So she enrolled at the campus in Iowa City and borrowed to the hilt.

I was like, 'Whatever,' she said. *I'll have four years to even think about paying loans. But then you see the numbers start to climb… and it's like, 'Wow!'*

After a single year at Iowa, she was $40,000 in debt.

She transferred to Parkland College and pursued an associate's degree in applied science.

After graduating in 2015, she quickly landed a job as a vet tech at the College of Veterinary Medicine at the University of Illinois.

Caitlyn was soon supervising the vet students in the anesthesiology department. She helped teach the future veterinarians about the proper ways to inject dogs, cats, pigs, horses and cows.

She still has the student debt in her way. To help pay it down, she has taken a second job as a bartender.

I'll be paying for a long time, she said.

But she loves the job, and she is optimistic about her career prospects.

Working at a teaching hospital, she said, *there's a lot of room for growth.*

For all the academic accomplishments of community college students, some of them still feel somehow second-class.

You know what saddened me when I worked at the community college? O'Keefe wrote in the *Motherlode* blog. *Overhearing or meeting students who sounded apologetic for being there. They had heard the message that community college was not real college, and they listened.*

So next time someone shares the news that they're going to community college, how about this? Tell them they are amazing. Tell them they have taken the first step to being a college graduate and that step can change their life.

Tell them you are proud of them.

CHAPTER SIXTEEN

BRINGING THE UNIVERSITY
TO THE WORKPLACE

Like a lot of other businesses, my company had a reimbursement program that helped employees with tuition costs. That was a nice benefit. But often it wasn't enough.

In a meeting with the management team at our headquarters in New Jersey in 2010, I issued a call to action: It was important to me that we do our best to provide free education to anyone in the company, from the CEO to the janitors.

Taking on college for a busy adult can be overwhelming. People with work and family demands are already feeling swamped. While trying to balance all of the usual duties, it can be awfully difficult to navigate the college admissions process, figure out class schedules that fit into busy lives, and find the time and energy to make the commute to a college campus a couple of times a week. We wanted to eliminate as many hurdles as possible.

We settled on an approach that one of our team members described as *a little bit radical.*

If going to college was an obstacle for our workers, we decided we would bring the college to our workers.

And so Heartland University was born.

In our model, it is the professors who would do the commuting. They came to our corporate service center and taught students in our classrooms. The employees could simply walk from their jobs to class.

The program allowed Heartland employees to enroll in programs to earn an associate's or a bachelor's degree in business administration. For the associate's degree track, we worked with Ivy Tech, the state-run community college system in Indiana. For the bachelor's program, we coordinated with the Indiana Institute of Technology, a private four-year institution based in Fort Wayne.

Classes were offered on Monday through Thursday evenings, as well as on Saturday mornings. We paid for all costs of books and tuition not already covered by financial aid. We handled the admissions paperwork and we provided tutors for any students who requested them. We eventually enrolled more than 100 students in Heartland University.

The college-at-the-office program cost us a bit over $100,000 a year. It was worth every penny.

Like the scholars in the Give Something Back Foundation, these were students who deserved a break. Many had been away from school for years. Going back to the classroom took courage. The average age at Heartland U was in the thirties. Some were over fifty.

At social gatherings, Ashley Wilson would grow uncomfortable when others shared small talk about their college days and majors.

Ashley would stay mum. She had no degree.

It can sometimes feel as though everyone has been through college. They haven't. The overwhelming majority of Americans do not have an associate's degree. But the lack of a college diploma deeply bothered Ashley.

She certainly didn't lack for drive or smarts. She was an excellent employee for Heartland in the company's service center in Jeffersonville, Indiana. When any Heartland customer around the country had a problem, these were the workers who took the calls.

It was Ashley's job to find answers. She was acing tests every day.

I was sure other people would wonder, 'So why don't you have a degree?' she said.

She often asked herself the same thing. Ashley decided to enroll in Heartland University.

Our incoming students often received a pep talk from Christopher Hargett, the director of training at Heartland and the manager of the college program.

They might be a little bit afraid, he said. *We tell them: 'Don't worry. You've shown you can work hard and you're smart. You can do it. And we're going to be there for you.'*

Our first graduating class for the associate's program walked across the commencement stage in May of 2015. On the eve of the ceremony, I took the grads and their families out to dinner and told them how much I respected the accomplishment.

I'm proud of you, I told them. I had a lump in my throat as I looked around the fancy restaurant at these modest, working-class families, beaming with pride over a feat many had never thought possible.

At age thirty-three, Ashley Wilson was one of the ten graduates in the inaugural Heartland class in 2015. As the first in her family to earn a college degree, she said she especially wanted to make an example for her two young children, Cohen, nine, and Joslin, five.

I did this for my kiddos, she explained. *They were absolutely my driving force.*

A few years earlier, Cohen had been struggling mightily in the first grade. He didn't want to go to school. He especially hated reading.

When Ashley went back to school, however, she began to see some changes in her son.

When he saw his mom with a book, doing her homework, it made a difference, she said. *And I told him, 'You can't quit. If I can do it, you can do it. We're both going to make it.'*

Cohen is now doing much better in school, and his sister, Joslin, who is in preschool, gets very excited to do homework and be *just like mom.*

Her supportive husband, Paul, who worked the night shift, did everything he could to help at home and he cheered Ashley every step of the way. It was a family team effort. The grandparents stepped in to help with care for the kids whenever needed.

Even with all the support, there were times when Ashley felt like giving up.

After rising at 6 a.m., and working all day, she was in class until after 9 p.m. twice a week. She felt swamped with homework, some of it very difficult. The work in the accounting class was daunting.

Late into the night, she would be making sandwiches for the kids for lunch for the next day and seeing to the other chores around the house. She was exhausted.

I couldn't focus, she said. *I was done. I told my husband, 'I can't do this for another two years.'*

He reminded her about all that was at stake, both for her own sense of pride, and for the lesson she was teaching Cohen.

You can do it, he told her. *We'll figure it out.*

She also credited coworkers with lifting one another up. These were teammates on the job, and now they were teammates in the classroom, too.

Teachers from Ivy Tech noted that having employees take classes on-site added a layer of accountability. In other words, the students worked hard to impress their teachers, as well as their colleagues and the management staff on the job.

We made sure to honor their accomplishments. In our internal communications, we publicized the names and pictures of those students who made the Dean's List. We celebrated milestones, such as the completion of each module, and we flew students from Indiana to the New Jersey headquarters to be honored at a lunch.

Ivy Tech believes our model could be replicated by many other employers. We think so, too. Unfortunately, the companies willing to make the financial commitment for on-site college education are few and far between.

We hope that changes. Our students learn a lot that helps them become more effective colleagues, almost immediately. Ashley Wilson, for example, had been putting her education to work from the start. In a business class, she said, she learned among other things that you don't have to be in management to be a leader.

You can lead peers by example, she said. *And you can speak up. You can open eyes.*

Her classes included business, quantitative reasoning, economics, marketing, and her dreaded accounting course, among others. As she faced the challenges in the classroom, she said, she could feel herself growing stronger and smarter.

I have a lot more confidence, said Ashley. *I can now understand the issues better and speak about them more effectively.*

On graduation day, Ashley's proud parents sent a bouquet of flowers to the office for her.

The 2015 commencement for Ivy Tech students from southern Indiana and Louisville was held at the Northside Christian Church in New Albany. It was a beautiful auditorium that seated a huge crowd. Three big screens flashed images of the grads in gowns and their families, many of them in tears.

A string quartet played classical music. The rows were festooned with white ribbons. Among the graduates at the ceremony, the ten Heartlanders sat together. And when they were called to the stage, they raised their arms in triumph.

Another new grad, Jen Taylor, thirty, said she had begun to see a new face in the mirror. A few years back, she had made some promises to herself. She was going back to school to earn a degree. And she was going to become active and healthy.

Every day during lunch, she would exercise in the Heartland gym with the company's personal trainer, Maggie. She had lost sixty pounds and was now running in 5K races. She had even signed up for something called Rugged Maniac, a three-mile obstacle course that involves crawling through mud, running through fire, climbing hills and scaling walls.

She had earned her associate's degree, and was moving straight into the bachelor's degree program.

I wanted more in my life, she said, *and everything fell into place.*

On the morning of commencement, Karri Lewis's husband, Kevin, had asked her what she wanted most as a gift for graduation.

I want my mom to be there, she told him.

Like many of the other Heartland employees, Karri was the first in her family to earn a college degree.

It's not about the piece of paper, she explained. *It's about the journey it took to get here.*

In 1981, the year before Karri was born, her mother, Donna, was diagnosed with muscular dystrophy at age twenty-five.

Her father would eventually leave his sick wife for another woman. Karri grew up watching her mother grow weaker and weaker. A woman who once walked five miles a day would eventually have trouble climbing a flight of stairs.

When Karri was nine years old, her mother started falling down frequently. Two years later, a terrible fall required surgery, and except for a few steps with a walker, she would never walk again.

Karri did not have much of a childhood. She was her mom's primary caregiver.

As a little girl, she hurried home to cook for her mother and help her get to the bathroom. Money was scarce, so when Karri reached high school, she took a full-time job on the night shift, clocking in at a grocery store after taking care of her mother until helping her into bed.

On many mornings, Karri went to school without having had a minute of sleep, either because she had been lying awake worrying about her mother, or because there was simply no time for rest.

Karri's father, meanwhile, stayed on the periphery of her life. His occasional presence was dictated, in large part, by the competing demands of his dating life. When he had a steady girlfriend, her dad would focus more time and energy on that woman's kids than his own.

He broke with Karri completely when she was eighteen. Karri had committed what her father believed to be an unforgivable sin. She had fallen in love with a black man.

To justify the bigotry, her dad (and her grandmother, too) quoted exhortations from *their own made-up bible,* as Karri put it, that prohibited *race-mixing.*

Karri stood firm. She told her father that if he could not accept her love for Kevin, a truck driver, then her dad was free to leave her life.

Karri's mom gave her daughter her unwavering support and embraced her loving son-in-law.

As Karri saw it, her mom taught her more than any school could ever teach. Her mother was in pain every day, but never complained. She had even pushed her daughter out of the house – as Karri was burdened with guilt about leaving her mom's side – telling her it was time to start her life.

Before long, her mom could no longer get out of a wheelchair on her own. A hydraulic device, called a Hoyer lift, was needed to move her to the bathroom. Her arms grew so weak it was difficult for her to feed herself or grasp a glass of water. Doctors said her condition would progressively weaken her muscles and eventually stop her heart.

She is my inspiration, said Karri. *Whenever I feel overwhelmed, I think of that woman, and I ask, 'Who am I to complain?' I mean… I can walk.*

As soon as she asked Kevin for her graduation gift, the two of them went out and splurged on a rental van that was equipped to lift a wheelchair. They delivered it to her mom and stepfather and told them they could use it for whatever she wanted.

Her mom arrived at Commencement early. That way, she could take in the atmosphere and catch a glimpse of her daughter in her cap and gown. Her mother was enduring extreme fatigue.

As Karri grasped her diploma, she peered into the crowd and spotted her mother, hanging tough as ever, watching from the wheelchair. In the moment of triumph, the eyes of both of the women were glistening.

Karri was walking across the commencement stage for both of them.

CHAPTER SEVENTEEN

SKILLED TRADES: THE OTHER COLLEGE

The nation's businesses have more than five million skilled labor positions going unfilled, according to the US Department of Labor, a startling number considering that so many Americans are out of work or underemployed.

The reason for this paradox is a skills mismatch. We don't train enough people for the talents now demanded in the country's increasingly sophisticated workplaces.

The typical manufacturing job, as an example, now takes far more than simple brawn or the patience to do repetitive tasks. It requires advanced technical training and critical thinking.

What keeps workers from learning the skills for well-paying jobs? It is often a combination of outdated thinking and elitism.

A public school counselor in Madison, Wisconsin, has seen plenty of it. Students demonstrate an aptitude in careers in technical skills and crafts, he said, but their vocational interests meet with resistance at home.

Their parents are horrified by the idea that their kids wouldn't go to a traditional four-year college, he said. *Some of the dads and moms are professors at the University of Wisconsin. If their kid wanted to go into a trade, they worry, 'What would people think?'*

As labor secretary, Thomas Perez spearheaded a campaign to encourage such skeptical parents to broaden their views.

Apprenticeships, he insisted, should not be considered as an alternative to an academic route. Instead, they should be viewed simply as the *'other college.'* It's the college that comes with a paycheck during schooling, a job offer afterward and the absence of debt.

What part of that, he has asked parents, *don't you like?*

While Americans tend to be familiar with apprenticeships in the building trades, such as carpentry, plumbing or masonry, they are often unaware of such programs in many other sectors. But companies now sponsor paid apprenticeships in fields such as information technology, health care, logistics and cybersecurity.

Some of these apprenticeships can lead to jobs that earn mid-career salaries in the neighborhood of $100,000, or even more.

Apprenticeships have a long and rich history in Europe, and such programs are on the rise among US companies. South Carolina, which has been aggressive in urging companies to develop apprenticeships, saw more than a seven-fold increase in businesses offering such programs in just a handful of years.

Apprenticeship programs throughout the nation are expected to see more vibrant growth in the years ahead, as changing technology in almost every sector plays an increasingly larger role.

A shortage in skilled workers prompted one North Carolina business to create an apprenticeship program starting in high school. When students complete the three-year program, they have an associate's degree and a position with a salary of $55,000.

The building trades, too, are leaning more heavily on apprenticeship programs. The apprenticeships were cut back during the housing collapse after 2008, but have grown since the recovery. Coupled with the retirement of many baby boom generation tradesmen, that means a lot of opportunity – wages of more than $40 an hour and benefits – for skilled journeyman.

This is not a path for slackers. Those interested in the apprenticeship path should recognize that academics and character play a key role. Many building trades unions and companies conduct random drug tests. Having so much as a beer at lunch is typically a firing offense.

Skills in mathematics, moreover, are a necessity. Winning a spot in an apprenticeship program typically requires passing a test, and about 50 percent fail the exam, according to Darren Bonass, a recruiter for union carpenters in Pennsylvania. For high school students who aspire to a career in the trades, that means it's important to study hard in math and other classes.

The old notion of a blue-collar worker simply being good with his hands never really made sense. My hands work very well. I type many thousands of e-mails on my computer every year. But that doesn't mean I could wire a house for electricity. For a talented trades worker, it is not the manual dexterity that counts, as much as the knowledge of how to create and make things work. A surgeon, after all, is a job that requires being good with your hands.

The idea that people necessarily pursue either an education or a trade has become both anachronistic and a false choice.

Williamson College of the Trades, near Philadelphia, combines vocational training and traditional academic subjects.

A student might specialize in carpentry or masonry or horticulture, but will also take classes in physics, chemistry and Spanish, as well as other subjects.

The three-year school offers free tuition, as well as room and board, for high-achieving young men from the Philadelphia area who have demonstrated financial need and good character. Enrollment has traditionally been around 265 students.

Regarded as one of the finest trade institutions of higher education in the nation, Williamson offers associate technology degrees. Some 70 percent go on to earn a bachelor's degree.

Some of them never grasped a hammer. Through instruction, study and practice, they learn to meet exacting standards. If the students in the masonry shop build a fireplace that is out of plumb, the want-to-be bricklayers are ordered to tear it down and begin again.

The code of conduct, meanwhile, is among the most rigorous of any institution in the country, including the armed services. The college enforces a zero tolerance policy for illicit alcohol or drug use, and a single lapse means the loss of a scholarship.

Of the Williamson students who enter a trade, 80 percent join the ranks of management within a decade of leaving school, often starting their own businesses.

Companies covet these students. When Williamson hosted its job fair in 2016, some 120 employers jammed the school's gymnasium for a chance to recruit the school's seventy-six seniors. It is not unusual for a student to receive a half-dozen or more job offers.

Kevin Leonard, a project manager who was representing a Philadelphia construction company, said flatly: *I would hire every student here.*

CHAPTER EIGHTEEN

DON'T BLAME THE KIDS

Children do not choose to live with poverty or abuse. Whatever one might think of judicial policies on incarceration, it is scarcely the fault of a child whose parent has been sent to prison. It is not the child who is to blame for being smuggled across the US border without documentation.

It should not be surprising when disadvantaged kids fall short or go astray. What *is* amazing – and truly inspiring – is how many rise up from difficult lives and go on to achieve success in the classroom and beyond. They have learned to draw on strengths borne of adversity and struggle.

In her competitive suburban high school in Plainfield, Illinois, about an hour west of Chicago, Leslie Juarez was a whiz on the mathematics team that qualified to go to state.

She was a star in Advanced Placement courses in biology, chemistry, physics, English, Spanish, government, US history, and her favorite subject, calculus.

In a class of more than 500, she was academically ranked number two.

Brilliant and engaging, a popular teenager with a million-dollar smile, she was seen as a girl who had it all.

No one knew that Leslie was harboring a secret. She did not have everything. She did not have US citizenship.

Scarcely a day passed that Leslie did not worry that this was the day that she and her parents would be deported and sent back to Mexico.

Like Leslie, more than one million minors living in the US were brought to this country by their parents or relatives.

In Illinois alone, about 1,300 undocumented students graduate from high school annually. Fewer than 10 percent of them go directly to college. Under law, no federal or state financial aid money can be granted to these students.

Some call them illegals. Leslie, like many other young immigrants, calls herself a DREAMer.

Born in the small Mexican town of Chaka in 1994, Leslie was only a toddler when her father sneaked across the border and made his way to Chicago. He found work as a cook in a Long John Silver restaurant. It was a job that paid far more than any wages he could earn in Mexico. It was his plan to work in the US for a few years and save money, then return to Mexico and build a house for the family.

As a little girl, Leslie missed her father deeply. She would gaze at his photograph, and one day, she discovered an identification card he had left behind. She wore it around her neck to feel closer to him.

When Leslie started school, she was told by her mother to say nothing about the whereabouts of her father. That could make them a target. People knew that those with jobs across the border typically sent money home to their families. Not far from Leslie's home, a woman and her two children had been robbed and killed by marauders looking for money and goods sent from a dad working in the US.

For a little girl, there were other things to fear, too. Children of single women were often stigmatized and teased about having no father at home. Some of the other kids taunted Leslie. One boy kicked her shins. Another lifted up her skirt to expose her underwear. The other children said Leslie was only making up a story about having a father.

Desperate to defend her parents, she took out her dad's identification card and showed it to them.

She remembers one boy laughing in ridicule.

You're a liar, he sneered. *Your mom's just a whore.*

She is not! Leslie shot back in a flash of anger. *I do have a dad. He lives in Chicago. He has a job as a cook… and he sends money and other things to us.*

When her mother found out about the exchange on the playground, she reprimanded Leslie.

Don't ever tell them that… it's too dangerous! Whatever they want to say about me… just let them say it!

Leslie was seven years old when her father returned home. He had saved money, but now he wanted something more than a nicer house for his family in Mexico. He wanted a better life for them in the US.

One momentous day, he announced, *Let's go.*

Her father had hired a *coyotaje*, or coyote, a person who helps smuggle migrants across the border.

Leslie's parents made plans for the escape. Her mom and dad would go ahead. Leslie and a young cousin would follow behind them. The little girls would be accompanied by a woman posing as their mother. The coyote had arranged for this fake mom and he had secured identification papers of two little girls whose size and age roughly matched Leslie and her cousin.

As they encountered the border patrol in Ciudad Juárez, agents grew suspicious. They told the girls to wait in a nearby office. They wanted to ask them a few questions.

The identification papers described Leslie's cousin as being seven years old. In truth, the girl was only five.

Remember, Leslie told the cousin as they waited for an agent to arrive to conduct the questioning, *you are seven years old… don't forget that!*

The little girl responded: *No, I'm only five. I don't want to lie.*

Leslie tried to reassure her: *You need to lie. It's okay this time.*

When the border patrol officer entered the room, he began to ask some questions to make sure their stories matched the information on the papers.

When Leslie's younger cousin was asked her age, she told the truth, that she was five. And then she was asked about her parents. The little girl gave their real names. The ruse was up.

The girls were sent to what Leslie described as a kind of an orphanage. She said the authorities told her they would send word to her dad, who was staying with her mom in El Paso, Texas, that the children were being detained, and he could come and pick them up.

Leslie remembers: *One of the kids in the orphanage said to me, 'It's a lie. The parents never come back.'*

Her dad did return, as she knew he would, and almost immediately, he outlined plans to make another run for El Norte.

At the edge of the Rio Grande, Leslie's dad tucked her and the younger cousin under each of his arms.

Leslie, who had learned to swim, told her father confidently: *I've got this. I can do it.*

But her dad wouldn't let go. And soon they were standing on the US side of the river.

They were picked up by a truck, arranged by the coyote, and they lay themselves down in the bed of the vehicle. The driver took them to a makeshift motel. Leslie said it was crawling with rats.

As they entered a room, Leslie saw her mom, ran to her and hugged her tightly.

They soon walked to a Kmart to buy some clothes, Leslie said, so that *we would look more American.*

Leslie said the coyotes even taught them how to walk so they wouldn't invite suspicion.

Mexican parents tend to hover over the children, she said. *They warned us not to do that. It would be a giveaway.*

From El Paso, the family flew to Chicago. They soon settled into an apartment on Clark Street. The bright lights and energy seemed thrilling to Leslie, who was used to the quiet, slow pace of her small town in Mexico.

Wow, she thought to herself, *this is a city!*

It did not take long, however, before her parents decided that the crime-ridden Chicago neighborhood was not the right place to raise a child. The breaking point came as they were walking to church, Leslie said, *to say happy birthday to Our Lady of Guadalupe.* A fight between rival gangs exploded nearby and gunshots were fired.

The family moved to a suburb outside Chicago, and then moved again to Plainfield, a small Illinois town at the edge of corn and bean fields.

It was in Plainfield that Leslie learned to speak English. She was one of a small number of Hispanic kids at the elementary school.

She was placed in an ESL class, short for English as a Second Language. Leslie was smart, ambitious, and she conceded, *a little bit stubborn.*

They gave me books in Spanish, she said, *and I gave them back and said, 'No, I want English.'*

Many exceptionally bright immigrant kids, like Leslie, are overlooked by schools when selecting students for classes geared to the gifted, since the aptitude tests are typically given only in English. In Leslie's case, her arrival in the United States at a relatively early age — and her unmistakable smarts — helped her eventually qualify for accelerated classes in high school.

Even among close friends, Leslie knew she had to stay *hush-hush* about her family being undocumented.

She remembers visiting the home of a friend, a boy she cared about very much, and she heard him utter a condescending reference to the family's housekeeper as an *illegal.*

What if you knew, she remembers thinking in silence, *that I'm actually 'one of them.'*

Such put-downs were commonplace. Leslie said that even some Mexican American people — those who had citizenship papers — would sometimes make hurtful comments about a mojado, a slur that translates to wetback.

When the rest of her high school classmates were making plans about college, Leslie made an appointment to talk to a guidance counselor.

Leslie shared her college and career aspirations. She spoke about her dream of becoming a veterinarian. She drew a breath, and then nervously explained that there was something else she needed to discuss. She was in the country illegally. It was the first time she had said it to anyone.

This was going to be a problem, her counselor told her, and suggested that Leslie scale back her ambitions.

Leslie was crushed. *I had worked so hard,* she said.

From the time she was little, she had learned how to navigate the system. In school, when a parent's signature was required to attest that a child had completed a homework task, Leslie would simply hand the form to her mother and tell her, *Just sign here. It says that you know I read the assignment.*

Leslie was not merely book-smart. By necessity, she had learned to become savvy in survival skills, from the playground in Mexico to the classroom in Plainfield.

Now she had come up against a barrier that seemed immovable.

It seems harsh to blame those, like Leslie, who were brought to the country as children, especially those who steered clear of trouble, worked hard in the classroom or served in the military.

In 2012, Leslie and others were given a break, when President Obama issued an executive action giving temporary legal protection to young immigrants under a program known as DACA, or Deferred Action for Childhood Arrivals.

To be eligible, immigrants needed to be younger than age thirty-one and have entered the United States before June 2007. They were required to be younger than sixteen years old when they arrived. They must have earned a high school diploma or a General Education Development (GED) certificate, be currently enrolled in high school, or have served honorably in the US armed forces.

Young immigrants do not qualify for the program if they have been convicted of a felony or a significant misdemeanor, such as a domestic battery or driving under the influence, or if they have been guilty of three misdemeanors of any kind.

The protection lasts for only two years at a time, and the program can be revoked by a new president with the stroke of a pen. Those conditions frighten away many young immigrants, who worry that signing up for the program leaves them more vulnerable to deportation if the measure is rescinded, since the authorities know about them.

Leslie was granted legal status under DACA, which gave her protection from deportation, at least temporarily, and allowed her to obtain a driver's license. That made it possible for her to get to her job and attend a technical school. She had enrolled in a program in the veterinary field, although it was not on the college track required to become a veterinarian.

Money was scarce. Leslie's parents were working four jobs between them. Her dad worked at two factories. Her mom worked at a McDonald's restaurant and at a grocery store in the produce department. Leslie worked, too. But her inability to qualify for federal and state aid seemed to slam shut the door to college.

On her drive home from work, she would pass by the University of St. Francis in Joliet, Illinois, and found herself admiring a beautiful old stone building on its campus. It was a former convent known as the Motherhouse, with a statue of a nun, Mother Alfred Moes, standing at the gate as a sign of welcome.

Despite all of the obstacles to going to college, something gave Leslie the idea that she should stop at this school. One day she pulled the car over and stepped along the walkway past the flowers and the welcoming statue of the sister, and pulled open the heavy door.

When she explained that she had some questions, she was steered to a student mentor.

Money was a problem, she explained. The mentor gave her a list of possible scholarships. Leslie shrugged and shook her head.

I can't apply for those scholarships, she said. *I'm a DREAMer.*

The student smiled back at her.

I'm a DREAMer, too, he said. He told her that she was welcome to apply for scholarships.

Call it divine inspiration, or just a happy coincidence, the University of St. Francis, she would learn, had taken a leading role among academic institutions in speaking up for immigrants and doing what was possible financially to help students without citizenship.

The president of the college was a man named Arvid Johnson, himself the descendant of immigrants from Sweden, Greece and Poland.

He said the school was honoring the tradition of the community of sisters who founded St. Francis nearly a century ago. The nuns had catered to women who were immigrants or were the daughters of immigrants. In later generations, the sisters of St. Francis were leaders in advocating for the rights of black and brown people. And he underscored that this Catholic school was proud of its tradition of reaching out to the poor and laboring classes of any background.

We don't care if you came without documents, he said.

At other schools, donors have raised eyebrows over any policy of granting admission and providing private scholarship money to students who did not have legal citizenship status. A few of the workers at St. Francis walked out of a session that included a panel of undocumented students describing their experiences.

But if anyone was skeptical, Johnson insisted, they would likely see it differently if they visited with one of the immigrant students.

I don't care how hard your heart is, said Johnson, a big man in a blue sport coat. *If you sit down for five minutes with one of these students, you'll understand why we're doing what we're doing. These are kids who don't get into trouble. They know what their parents have done to get them here.*

Scholarship aid from the university helped make it possible for Leslie to enroll at St. Francis, one of our partner schools. She majored in biology, with a double minor in chemistry and Spanish. Through her junior year, she posted a gaudy 3.8 grade point average.

She did plenty outside of the classroom, too. She mentored a student from the Middle East. She served as president of the school's multicultural club, United We Stand.

The University of St. Francis in 2016 hosted its second "Sharing the Dream" conference, which draws guidance counselors and teachers from throughout the nation to talk about the needs of immigrant children.

Roberto Gonzales, a Harvard professor, spoke at the initial conference about how undocumented children transition to adulthood and *awaken to a nightmare*.

Confronted by legal barriers and ineligible for many opportunities, Gonzales said, these students *find themselves stuck and on the outside looking in.*

An organizer of the conference, Eric Ruiz is the associate director of undergraduate admissions at St. Francis.

We train high school counselors about how to help undocumented students come out to them, he said.

Leslie has appeared at a panel during the conferences to talk about her journey, a story that has touches of humor.

When her family left Mexico, she said, she was forced to leave behind her two beloved dogs. Years later, when a family friend qualified for papers to come to the US, she brought along the dogs for Leslie.

I tell people that I came here illegally, she said, *but my dogs had visas.*

Even now, however, there is still a lot of worry in her voice when she talks about her parents, who work and live in the shadows.

You always have to worry that there will be a raid and they will be deported, she said trembling, as she explained why she worked so hard to achieve in school and why she felt such a driving obligation to aspire to a successful career.

I am here – in every way – because of my parents, she said in a quavering voice as she wiped away tears. *Everything I do is for them. I hope to give back.*

Before she could pose for a family photo with Santa Claus, four-year-old Shaleeka Page needed to remove her shoes and extend her arms, so that guards at the Pontiac Correctional Institution could pat her down for weapons or other contraband.

For Shaleeka, this was the earliest memory of going to see her father.

She remembers the long ride from her home on the South Side of Chicago. The drive stretched down city streets, beyond the suburbs and through vast open stretches of icy farm fields in downstate Illinois, until finally, she and her mom, Stacy, arrived at a massive fortress with a watchtower and high fences topped with razor wire.

I was wearing my brown overalls that day, Shaleeka recalled, now two decades later.

For a child who grew up seeing her dad so seldom, every detail was searing.

Some 2.7 million children in the United States have a parent in jail, according to the Pew Research Center, and about ten million kids have endured losing a parent to incarceration at some point in their lives. In Pennsylvania, for instance, almost as many young people have parents behind bars as there are students in all of that state's public universities.

These children face obstacles that are often even more damaging than those that come with losing a parent through death or divorce. Besides experiencing the trauma of the arrest itself – many prisoners were handcuffed in view of their children – these kids typically endure financial struggle, a lack of guidance, a measure of stigma and a sense of shame.

The children of incarcerated parents usually have fewer financial resources and less parental guidance. They are significantly more likely to suffer attention deficit, depression, anxiety, anger and even asthma, according to the American Academy of Pediatrics.

For much too long, innocent children have been invisible, silent victims of crime because their parents are incarcerated, wrote

Anna Hollis, the executive director of Amachi Pittsburgh, a group that provides mentoring to kids with mothers and fathers in jail.

Not surprisingly, their education often suffers. Among children with an incarcerated father, as few as 13 percent will graduate from any kind of college, according to a 2013 report by the American Bar Association and the White House. For kids with a mother behind bars, the report found, the rate of college graduation is between 1 and 2 percent.

More often than not, these children have little or no contact with a jailed parent. According to the Sentencing Project, more than half of parents in state prisons have never had a visit from a child.

In the case of Shaleeka, several months, and sometimes years, would pass without her seeing her father. When he was housed in prisons in distant regions, some six or seven hours away, it was simply too expensive for her mother to afford the gas and motel tab for a long trip.

To address the sense of despair and isolation that afflicts so many kids of jailed parents, Amy Friedman founded a group at a Los Angeles high school known as Pain of the Prison System, or POPS. When the prison gate slams shut, the children left behind are what Friedman calls *the collateral damage*.

On the first Monday of each month, as many as sixty students with incarcerated family members gather in a classroom at the school to share lunch and talk about their experiences in one of the few social settings that seem safe to open up.

Most kids feel it has to be kept secret, said Ms. Friedman, herself the mother of two children who have endured the imprisonment of their father, her ex-husband. *If you have to keep everything a secret all the time, it makes everything else in school a lot harder.*

Sites on Facebook also allow children of jailed parents to reach one another, share experiences and offer one another support.

Shaleeka's parents, Stacy and Johnny Page, were sixteen and eighteen, respectively, when she was born in Chicago in 1991. A month later, her father was sent to jail for street gang trouble.

From an early age, Shaleeka was whip-smart, a kid who could read fluently in preschool. But almost as soon as she knew her father was in prison, her mom says, the little girl grew angry at the world.

As a kid in elementary school, she daydreamed about what life would be like if her father were free, and she cherished the painfully brief conversations on the telephone with her dad.

He would tell me it wasn't my fault that he wasn't around, that he was the one to blame, she said. *There were times we'd get into such good talks, or we'd get to laughing, and then a voice would come on the line and say, 'You have one minute left.'*

She and her dad had a rule. They would never say goodbye. That seemed too final. Instead, her father would finish the conversation with the words, *I love you, Angel,* and she would respond, *I love you, too, Daddy.*

The little girl made it her mission to rescue her father. *When I was young,* she said, *I would tell people that when I grow up, I'm going to be a judge, so I can get my daddy out of jail.*

As Shaleeka grew into adolescence, and endured the consequences and shame of a jailed father, she would grow angry at the world.

Over the phone, her father offered advice.

Control the moment… don't let the moment control you,
he would tell her.

But Shaleeka's temper and fighting worsened. Punishment and suspension from school became routine.

She eventually grew resentful of her father, too. There were times she became livid that he even dared to give her advice.

Who are you to tell me how to live my life? she would scream at her father through the phone. *You're not here where I need you. You're in jail!*

After such an outburst, there would be silence on the phone for long moments, and then her dad would speak in a small voice that was etched with shame.

You're right, he acknowledged.

Her anger escalated toward her mother, too, a phenomenon that is not uncommon in cases when a dad is absent. Mothers are obligated to make the world right for a child, after all, and when life is unfair, Mom is somehow to blame.

At home, Shaleeka snapped at her mother so much that she eventually moved out and lived with her grandmother. At school, Shaleeka talked back to authority figures, as she put it, *just because they were authority figures.*

And then Shaleeka turned inward, her mother recalled.

She just began to shut down, her mom said. The girl would rarely speak. Instead, she used her fists to communicate.

Shaleeka fought with girls and she fought with boys. Kids often act toughest when they are feeling weakest and most vulnerable, and this was a kid hiding inside some very heavy armor.

People would tell me that I was just like my dad, Shaleeka said. *And I knew they didn't mean it as a compliment.*

By the time she was in the eighth grade, she had changed schools six times. In her freshman year at Dunbar Vocational High School, she failed every class.

She switched to Senn High School, and then transferred again, to Hyde Park Academy. At seventeen, she had a baby.

Completing her education, it became clear, was looking like a very long shot. A guidance counselor even advised her to quit school, saying there was no chance that she could catch up and graduate.

Shaleeka seized on her impulse to fight – but this time, she fought to prove herself in the classroom.

With the help of another guidance counselor, who was more encouraging, she made a long list of the classes she would need to complete in order to graduate.

The schedule seemed to be the length of a marathon. Shaleeka ran it like a sprinter. From Monday through Friday, she attended classes from 8 a.m. to 9 p.m. On Saturday morning, she attended school until noon.

Her mother would be waiting in the car to pick her up from one school and take her to the next, racing to the makeup courses she needed to complete after regular school hours. Each extra class cost a fee. Shaleeka's mom dug deep to pay for them.

Shaleeka pushed so hard, going to classes, studying almost nonstop and caring for her baby after hours, that she came home one evening and collapsed in tears, nearly paralyzed with exhaustion and anxiety.

I can't do this anymore! she wept.

Yes, her mother implored. *You can!*

The next morning, Shaleeka was back in the classroom, fighting to stay awake, and determined to keep chasing her diploma.

Nearly half of her Hyde Park class would fail to make it to the graduation stage. Many dropped out, others failed, some wound up in jail. Two classmates were killed by gunfire.

Shaleeka made it to commencement. As soon as she heard the first strains of "Pomp and Circumstance," tears began to rush down her cheeks. Her mom cried, too. Her grandmother and her relatives watched and wept – and they cheered.

I felt so proud, Shaleeka said.

With hopes of becoming a nurse, Shaleeka enrolled in Kennedy-King College in Chicago. She left after a year. Her debt was growing. She was working full-time at the Glen Elston Nursing Home. And she soon became the mother to a second child.

She earned $10.50 an hour as an aide at the nursing home, and lived paycheck to paycheck. She was looking forward to receiving about a thousand dollars as a tax refund, but the government seized it to apply against her outstanding student debt.

She still planned to return to college. She wanted to earn a bachelor's degree. It was her goal to become a registered nurse.

Shaleeka knew the odds were against her. But she had watched someone she loved climb out of a much deeper hole.

It was in prison that her father, Johnny Page, became a college student.

Johnny was eight years old when his own dad was gunned down, and the little boy watched helplessly as his mother's drug addiction worsened.

By the time he was eleven or twelve, he joined a street gang. Like a lot of lost boys, he realized later, he was looking for acceptance and validation – a family of sorts – that cared enough to fight for him.

We all want to belong to something, right? he said.

In the '80s, cocaine began to flood the streets of Chicago, and there was money to be made.

You'd see high school kids, Johnny recalled, *driving around in Cadillacs.*

When he was fourteen, Johnny started selling drugs himself, peddling a form of crack known in Chicago as ready rock. And he tried to style himself as a young gangster.

I had the street starter kit, he said, ruefully, *chains and anything Nike.*

He had been a good student through elementary school, but now his grades began to slide. At fifteen, he started packing heat. He acquired his first gun in a trade for drugs. When police arrested him not long afterward, he had his weapon, some drugs and a big roll of bills in his pocket. He was sent to the old Audy Home, a former juvenile detention center in Chicago, and then to a jail for minors in suburban St. Charles.

When he was released to the streets, he wasted no time getting back into the action. At age seventeen, he nearly died in the trauma unit of Northwestern Memorial Hospital after five gunshots pierced his back, stomach and hip in gang warfare. When he recovered and returned to the South Side, he discovered he had earned a gaudy – and exaggerated – reputation on the streets.

I was seen as a 'bad ass,' he recalled, *a 'hood legend,' you know… the 'big homie.'*

Both the Chicago police and rival gangs knew the name Johnny Page. It was not long after that he was questioned in connection with a murder and released. Two weeks later, he was charged with the killing. It was a murder he insists he did not commit.

I know, 'That's what they all say,' he said, acknowledging that most would be skeptical of his claim. *But I've got no reason to lie now. I've done my time. If anything, I could probably have had my sentence reduced if I said that I did do it. But I can look you in the eye and promise you that I did not kill that man.*

But he does not consider himself innocent, either.

I do feel responsible, he said. *I was part of that street madness. I helped create that virus. My cousin died five years after I went to prison, and I feel responsible for his death. He followed me into the streets.*

Johnny was sent to a maximum security penitentiary in Pontiac, a prison known by inmates as the Thunderdome, for its riotous, hellhole reputation. After he arrived, he remembers being led past cellblocks jammed with prisoners shouting catcalls at the incoming *fresh meat.*

He would spend the next twenty-three years behind bars, with transfers to a half-dozen penitentiaries in the state.

Along the way, one older inmate gave some unsolicited advice: *Go to school.*

Johnny initially shrugged it off.

I just want to be left alone.

The older inmate didn't give up.

Challenge your thinking, he told the young man.

At first, said Johnny, *I thought, 'What the hell is that supposed to mean?'*

But he did enroll in a class. And he soon became a voracious reader.

My life was changed by reading 'The Fountainhead' and Plato's 'Allegory of the Cave,' he said. *I began to understand the meaning of 'challenging your thinking.'*

He found resonance in Plato's prisoners, chained in place and staring at the shadows on the wall. Johnny decided he would turn away and face the sun of truth, just as the philosopher had described.

Reading changed the way I saw the world, he said. *Even though I was still in prison, I became free. I knew that I would never again fit as a gang member.*

Johnny spent his last prison years in Danville Correctional Center. It was there that he saw a sign for the Education Justice Project, one of the relatively small number of programs in the country that offered for-credit, upper-level college courses.

Danville, a medium security prison in a tiny town near the Indiana border, about 150 miles south of Chicago, houses some 1,800 men, 18 percent of them convicted of murder.

The college-in-prison program was founded and directed by Rebecca Ginsburg, a University of Illinois professor. Born to a Jewish father and a black mother, Ginsburg grew up in Canada and was raised in the Quaker tradition. She was living proof that it's not easy to put someone into a tidy category with an easy label. She made it her business to see others in the same multidimensional way.

With a law degree from the University of Michigan and a doctorate in architectural history from Berkeley, her interest in prison education went back to her days as a graduate student in California in 1997. As a volunteer instructor for inmates at San Quentin, she witnessed the obvious intelligence of many inmates, and saw firsthand how education could change seemingly doomed lives.

About 2.2 million people are now incarcerated in the United States. About 95 percent of them will reenter society. According to the Bureau of Justice Statistics, some 77 percent will be arrested again at some point – a majority of them within five years of release.

In New York, as an example, it costs $60,000 a year to house an inmate, according to a 2016 editorial by the *New York Times*. For that sum, the Give Something Back Foundation provides full-ride, four-year college scholarships for three students.

Research shows convincingly that two factors mostly determine whether inmates will succeed on the outside after release: a transformed character and a marketable skill.

A Rand Corporation study in 2013 found that inmates who took any college-level class were 43 percent less likely to wind up returning to prison after release. For every $1 spent on educating inmates, between $4 and $5 dollars are saved on reincarceration costs, Rand found.

But policies of the last two decades have sharply curtailed efforts to educate inmates. In 1993, some 23,000 prisoners were recipients of Pell Grants. The following year, Congress passed a bill that eliminated those grants. In New York alone, the number of inmates earning college degrees fell from 1,078 in 1991 to 141 in 2011.

At a time when a college degree is the basic price of admission to the information economy, the *New York Times* noted in 2016, *more than 40 percent of inmates lack a high school diploma.*

Fewer than fifty of the nation's roughly 1,800 state and federal prisons offer a program to teach college-level classes to inmates. The program in Danville, which began in 2008, is a rare program that offers inmates the opportunity to complete for-credit University of Illinois studies through the junior year of college.

In the decade since the program began, the recidivism rate stood at 8 percent for those Danville inmates who took the University of Illinois classes before being released to society.

As Ginsburg sees it, when inmates become serious about their studies, they look at themselves differently. The narrative of their lives and identities begins to change.

My brother now brags about me, she said one prisoner told her.

Ginsburg also holds get-togethers in Chicago for the families and loved ones of the prisoners in Danville. It has been her mission to foster stronger family ties, as well as create a support network among people with an incarcerated relative. Those who meet at her conferences frequently make arrangements to carpool to Danville, sharing the costs of a trip that might otherwise be too expensive.

Perhaps most important, she delivers positive updates on the progress of the inmates taking classes.

I don't know what he got locked up for, but I do know that he got an A in his last course, she has told the family member of an inmate. *I know that he's a leader and a caring person and you should be proud of him.*

More than once, a mother has responded to Ginsburg with tears and gratitude.

The mother will say, 'You're describing him the way I described him as a kid... thank you so much for telling me that.'

She also reaches out to young relatives, encouraging them to think seriously about school.

Your granddad is a University of Illinois student, she told one young boy who needed a supportive word. *What are your college plans? I hear you're really smart, too.*

The instructors at Danville have volunteered their time. They even pay for the gas needed to make trips to prison and back. Some of the volunteers are professors and instructors at Illinois. One of them, Sarah Lubienski, grew up in a trailer park and watched a family member go to jail.

Other volunteers come from outside academia. John Deckert, who grew up on the South Side of Chicago and earned a law degree at Notre Dame, has a practice in wealth management.

I work with rich people all day, he said. Spending his Friday nights teaching a finance class to inmates, he said, was a way *to keep me grounded.*

In a cinder block room with a chalkboard at the Danville prison, a University of Illinois pennant hangs on the wall. Nearly a dozen inmates sat around a rectangular table in the room and talked about their path toward an education.

One man recounted how he suffered a panic attack the first time he attended an information session about the college program. It had been years since he had been around anyone from the outside, he said, and he was terrified that he wouldn't know how to communicate with the civilian volunteers.

I started sweating real bad, said the inmate. He had been locked up for twenty years. An inmate sitting nearby saw his fright and whispered in his ear. *He said, 'Just listen, that's all you have to do.' And so that's what I did.*

Despite his nervousness, he signed up for the class. Through studying, he eventually found a sense of calm. He went on to complete four courses. His confidence improved so significantly that he served as the emcee at one of the information sessions.

Another inmate, a man with a long ponytail, said the classes had given his life meaning. *I live for it,* he said. *That's how important it is to me.*

One man, in a voice trembling with emotion, spoke about an essay he had written that was published in a college journal.

Most of us are guys who have never been applauded or awarded, he said. *In these classes, our voice matters. When my article was published, I was so proud. I take it out and read it sometimes and I think, 'Man, I did this!'*

Johnny Page walked out of Danville on September 26, 2014. Among his belongings was a poem he had written behind bars. It read in part:

'Nature or nurture, that is the question posed
An arduous task more suited to prose
So I guess you'll have to wait if you wish to see
If my life is less about the beginning and more about
What I make it to be.'

He returned to Chicago and reunited with Shaleeka and his two little grandchildren. He got a job at an organization called CeaseFire, which works to curb gang violence. He led a group of fifteen poor Chicago children on a trip to the University of Illinois. He explained that he had never set foot on a campus as a kid. He wanted them to know more about the possibilities of life with an education.

Put your names on the university mailing lists, he told them, *so that they'll send you things to make you think about college.*

And he enrolled in college himself. At Danville, he had completed enough courses to qualify as a second-semester junior. In January of 2015, he entered Governors State University, south of Chicago. He majored in psychology.

With a backpack slung across his shoulder, Johnny became a fixture in the evenings at the college library. With full-time work during the day and school in the evenings, he has sometimes become so weary he has fallen asleep in his parked car.

What goes around, he believes, comes around. So he makes time to volunteer at a food pantry.

At some points in my life, I have benefited from a food pantry, he said. *I have to give back.*

On a Saturday morning in May, with his family watching, Johnny Page walked across the commencement stage at Governors State University.

Shaleeka has promised to follow him.

CHAPTER NINETEEN

MAKING IT THROUGH AND GIVING BACK

———————————— ≈ ————————————

Good kids – smart kids – make mistakes. Too often, they end up paying the price for the rest of their lives. And society pays, too.

Adrianna Martinez is proof that it's worth sticking up for a kid who is in trouble.

In the summer after her eighth grade year, Adrianna had kept her secret as long as she could. Finally, she could wait no longer. Trembling with fear and shame, she sat down with her parents.

I'm pregnant, she told them.

Adrianna was thirteen years old.

Her mom, Raquel, and her dad, Jay, were devastated. There were expressions of disbelief, raised voices, talk of bitter disappointment, some angry words, and plenty of tears.

More than anything, they were scared – the parents and Adrianna alike.

For a few days, her parents were so upset with their daughter that they could barely speak to her.

Adrianna's mom had been a teenage mom herself. She had long vowed that history would not repeat itself. The cycle would be broken. To Raquel and Jay, this news meant great worry for the family, and embarrassment.

But for all of the worry and heartache, Raquel and Jay never stopped loving their daughter. And it soon dawned on them that they were voicing the same scorn and disapproval they that had heard themselves when they were young and in trouble.

So when their tears stopped – or at least slowed – they went to Adrianna and told her:

We are going to be in your corner. You can count on us. We will handle this together.

They had wanted so fervently to see Adrianna continue to succeed in her classes, go on to graduate from high school and then head out to college. They were not about to give up on the dream. They were not about to give up on their daughter.

But there was no escaping the harsh reality. The pregnancy would complicate a situation for a family that was already facing some daunting economic challenges.

The Martinezes lived south of Chicago in the town of Hazel Crest, an economically struggling community with a large population of black and Latino families. Adrianna's mom was Mexican American. Her dad was of Puerto Rican and Polish heritage. These were people who were fighting from week to week to pay the bills and keep the checks from bouncing. They didn't have money left over for big college costs.

When Adrianna became a freshman at Lockport Township High School, she joined a student body that seemed largely affluent and white. In her old neighborhood, she knew from experience, kids worked behind the counter at McDonald's or clerked at Louis Joliet Mall because they needed money. A lot of the kids at Lockport High, on the other hand, tended to be financially comfortable enough to devote their free time to playing sports or taking advantage of cultural enrichment activities.

One thing became quickly evident: Lockport was not a school accustomed to visibly pregnant girls walking the halls.

Adrianna gave birth to Ian Martinez on February 22, 2012. The new mom had just started the second semester of her freshman year of high school. At fourteen, she was not yet old enough to have a driver's permit, let alone a license. Not yet a year out of Chaney-Monge Elementary School, Adrianna would have to grow up in a hurry.

She learned some hard lessons about human nature, fickle friends and harsh judgment. After she became pregnant and then gave birth, many of her old pals and classmates started to steer clear of her.

I would talk to them at school, said Adrianna, *but whenever I tried to make plans with them, they were always busy.*

Were her old friends being warned by their parents to stay away from this *bad kid?* Or did her friends simply find it a drag to hang out with a girl caring for a crying baby? It was difficult to know.

All I knew was that they used to spend time with me, and now they didn't, said Adrianna, a soft-spoken, slender girl with straight black hair and glasses, who fought back tears when recalling the growing distance with some of her old friends.

She worried, too, about how she would ever be able to afford to go to college. Adrianna was familiar with the bleak statistics about teen moms. Only 40 percent of teenagers with a baby graduate from high school, according to studies compiled by the National Conference of State Legislatures, and only 2 percent of teenage mothers go on to graduate from college by age thirty.

Adrianna was even younger than most teen moms when she gave birth. But she wasn't going to give up. She relied on help from her parents to figure out a way to make school and young motherhood somehow work. She hit the books hard. And it paid off.

In her sophomore year, this young mom, a very bright student – and a good kid – finally caught a break. The Give Something Back Foundation awarded her a college scholarship.

There were strings, as there were for every one of the foundation's scholars. She would need to enroll in the kind of rigorous courses required to prepare her for college admission. She needed to maintain at least a 3.0 grade point average throughout high school. She would need to meet regularly with a mentor and attend the requisite foundation activities. And she would be required to demonstrate good behavior while at school and upstanding citizenship when away from campus.

Adrianna met the challenges. She took Advanced Placement courses in US history, biology, chemistry and French, among other courses. She earned all As and Bs, and she was selected to membership in the French National Honor Society.

It was in French class that Adrianna found a valued mentor in her teacher, Tina Sochacki.

Some teachers are there just to be teachers, Adrianna said. *But she could talk with me about out-of-school stuff – whatever was going on in my life. She was very supportive.*

As Adrianna saw it, having a mentor and being chosen for a scholarship pushed her toward academic excellence in two ways. It was a vote of confidence in her smarts. And it provided a stark reminder that she would be held accountable for her performance in the classroom and outside it.

When I felt like I didn't want to do schoolwork, I did it anyway, because I knew that if my grades slipped, I'd lose my scholarship, she said. *And I wanted to make sure I made choices that wouldn't disappoint anyone on the scholarship committee.*

Most child experts will tell you that kids, no matter what they say, desire structure, rules, a sense of order and the assurance that they will be treated with fairness for their actions. They also want someone to believe in them.

The Give Something Back scholarship gave her that boost of confidence – and the high bar of expectations.

It's a fundamental premise of the foundation: If we don't demand accountability from students, we are not doing them any favors. We are just selling them short.

Diluting standards for working-class kids, or those of color, moreover, can be a slippery slope of condescension that extends into bias in the job market. An employer would never say as much, but some worry about elevating someone to a position that seems beyond their comfort level.

These students *can* compete. They *can* lead. They *can* triumph. *And they do.*

Adrianna learned plenty about going beyond her comfort level. She understood that raising Ian and staying in school would mean a lot of work and some serious sacrifices. Through her middle school years, she had played the saxophone. Now with a baby, there wouldn't be much time for extracurricular activity.

In high school, her day started at 5 a.m., when she rose to get herself ready, dress Ian and prepare him for a child care center near her home called TLC.

She needed every penny she could scrape together.
In her junior year, she worked at the Family Fun Zone. In her
senior year, she worked fifteen hours a week making salads at a
restaurant called Merichka's.

Adrianna was able to network with other scholars in the
Give Something Back Foundation. She and the other scholarship
kids visited college campuses, gathered for the annual dinners at
DiNolfo's, and took the prep course we offer for the ACT college
entrance exam.

She took the exam in the second semester of her senior year.
She waited anxiously in the next weeks for the mail to come with
the results. She had earned good grades. A high score on the
ACT would help her win entry to a very good college.

On the day the mail carrier brought an envelope with ACT
marked in the corner, she trembled. She was so nervous she
asked her mother to open the envelope.

Her mom ripped it open, looked at the score, then let out a
scream. Now Adrianna looked, too. She gasped. The cumulative
score was a 31. That put her in the 97th percentile of all students!

It was a remarkable achievement. Her mother had done
some research on the test scores and what they meant. She knew
that a score nearing 30 would mean some merit aid – and
Adrianna had exceeded that threshold.

The mom and daughter jumped and hugged and cried.
It was one of the happiest, proudest days for her and her parents.
Little Ian, now three years old, could not have known quite what
caused all the joyous commotion in their little house that day.
But he surely knew that his mom and grandparents were awfully
happy. And so he was happy, too.

On a Saturday in June, Adrianna's parents held a high school graduation party. It was a double celebration. Adrianna had graduated from Lockport Township High School, and her younger brother, Vincent, had graduated from the eighth grade.

It was a festive crowd. Her Grandma Rachel, who lived two blocks away, was there, along with Great-Grandma Maria, and Aunt Lynette, who drove down from Chicago. Her brothers, Roberto and Will, were there to celebrate, too. And her best friend, Alex, who had stuck with her through thick and thin, walked through the door with a big smile. He wouldn't have missed the party for anything.

Ian was so excited, he had woken early that morning. He'd been told to get ready for a party. So he told Adrianna, *Happy Birthday, Mom!* He had the right idea.

But for a girl who entered high school with the odds so greatly stacked against her, this was a way bigger deal than any birthday party.

The Martinezes served food in two shifts, since many of the friends and family had to work part of the day on Saturday. Her mom had prepared pot roast and macaroni for the early shift, and chicken and corn for the latecomers.

For graduation presents, Adrianna received gift cards for bed sheets and other things she would need for her college dorm.

Adrianna chose to enroll at North Central College, a highly respected liberal arts college in Naperville, Illinois. It was about a forty-five-minute drive from home, so Adrianna would be able to come home frequently to see Ian. She would also work a shift on Sundays at Marichka's restaurant to help her earn some spending money.

To be able to get back and forth, she planned to take the family's lone car, an old Ford Escort that had been breaking down quite a bit. Her mother worked with her sister, so the two of them could ride together. Her dad, a mechanic, had been laid off from his job, so he didn't need a car just at the moment. One way or another, the Martinez family knew they could figure it out. They had overcome bigger challenges.

On a glorious summer morning, Adrianna and her parents pulled up to the campus of North Central College for freshman orientation. She glanced across the verdant and leafy campus – the stately old buildings, football stadium, a soaring church steeple on the horizon and young students on the sidewalks, marching ahead with their backpacks and a sense of purpose. It seemed to her like the land of promise.

With wide eyes and a nervous smile, Adrianna walked through the majestic doors of the orientation center at Wentz Concert Hall, a striking edifice of stone and glass.

On the wall, an old plaque and a photograph from long-ago alums welcomed them with the printed greeting: *Hail! Hail!*

The loudspeakers were playing an inspirational old Motown song, as the voice of Diana Ross sang: *Ain't no mountain high enough, Ain't no valley low enough*…. It could have been the anthem of Adrianna's nothing-can-stop-me spirit of making it in the world of higher education. She went on to sail through her first year of college with excellent marks.

Back in Will County, meanwhile, was a tenth grade girl in need of a mentor's help. Adrianna raised her hand to volunteer. She was grateful to have been given a break. Now it was time for her to give something back.

ROBERT OWEN CARR

EPILOGUE

Why make a mission of helping working-class kids reach college and the commencement stage? It's a question I'm often asked.

It is certainly not because I am selfless. I think we all do things largely because they bring us meaning, joy and gratification.

This is what makes me feel good. I have been fortunate enough to have the opportunity to change lives through education.

How cool is that?

In the beginning of our program, back in 2003, we could fit all of our scholars and their families at a couple of tables. At our most recent annual dinner for new scholarship recipients and other members of the Give Something Back family, there were 899 of us. And that was just for those in Illinois. We now also have scholarship students and families in New Jersey, Pennsylvania, Delaware and New York.

As I gazed out into the crowd at the Illinois gathering, I could see the smiling faces of the newly chosen ninth graders who earned scholarships. These were kids growing up in homes without extra money for college, and I saw a certain newfound confidence in these smart, hardworking young individuals who had found an entranceway on the path to upward social mobility.

But I was even more touched, I confess, when I looked at the parents, grandparents, even the siblings, and I saw such unmistakable and justified pride. For those who struggled to steer a kid toward the right path, the moment is truly sweet.

'That's my son or daughter or grandchild, the scholar!'

'Hey, look at what my brother or sister did!'

While Give Something Back initially worked with a single school, Lockport Township High School, we have lately grown at a very swift pace. The foundation has now paid for nearly 1,000 scholarships for working-class kids. I have contributed more than $25 million to the cause, and some generous donors are joining to help, too.

Our growing roster of partner colleges now includes schools in Illinois, Delaware, New Jersey, Pennsylvania and New York: Lewis University, University of St. Francis, Blackburn College, Northern Illinois University, the University of Illinois, the University of Delaware, the College of New Jersey, Montclair State University, Rowan University, Saint Peter's University, William Paterson University, New Jersey Institute of Technology, Williamson College of the Trades and Mercy College.

Snider Hockey's successful program reaches disadvantaged kids in Philadelphia. Through the sport of hockey, they provide a wonderful network of support for girls and boys. We are proud to partner with them in 'Goals and Assists,' an effort to help these students attend postsecondary institutions and graduate debt-free.

There are so many kids who deserve a hand. Give Back is now working with social service agencies in New Jersey to provide mentoring to students in foster care, many of them the sons and daughters of incarcerated parents.

Not long ago, I met with a group of thirty foster kids. I told them they would be receiving college scholarships. Afterwards, one of the recipients who spoke to the group described it as *forever a day that everyone in this room will remember for years to come.*

I know I will never forget the sentiments in her comments. She said that she and her foster peers had faced different obstacles, but that they shared one challenge in common: *How are we going to pay for college?*

In her talk, she painted this picture:

We live off stipends from the state, food stamps, and in cramped rooms. It takes a little extra for each one of us to get through our days. At school we see the kids with their designer clothes who couldn't fathom the climb we go through each day. We've reached false peaks way too many times to have the people in our lives break the promise that meant so much to us.... To have a miracle man reach down when our rope is running out, tired from holding on to anything we can grasp, it's nice to be lifted by that and to hear him say, 'Here, let me show you the way.'

I am not a miracle man. But I can assure this heroic girl of one thing: *This is a promise that will not be broken.*

We want to change the world – one working-class kid at a time.

For anyone who would like to join us as a donor or mentor, contact us at giveback.ngo.

INDEX

Also by ROBERT OWEN CARR with DIRK JOHNSON

*Through the Fires: An American Story of Turbulence,
Business Triumph and Giving Back*